The Need for Instruction . . .

Priests, both secular and religious, who are already working in the Lord's vineyard are to be helped by every suitable means to understand ever more fully what it is that they are doing when they perform sacred rites; they are to be aided to live the liturgical life and to share it with the faithful entrusted to their care.

With zeal and patience, pastors of souls must promote the liturgical instruction of the faithful, and also their active participation in the liturgy both internally and externally, taking into account their age and condition, their way of life, and standard of religious culture.

(*Vatican II, Constitution on the Sacred Liturgy,* nos. 18. 19.)

*   *   *

What must we do on this special and historic occasion [of the introduction of the new Mass rite]? Most important of all: we must prepare ourselves for it. This new rite is not something slight. We must not be surprised by the appearance, and possibly the complexity, of its external forms. As intelligent persons and conscientious Christians we must thoroughly inform ourselves about the new rite. This will be made easier by the ecclesial and publishing means that exist today.

(Allocution of Pope Paul VI, Nov. 26, 1969.)

THE
NEW MASS

A Clear and Simple Explanation
of the Mass as Restored and Renewed
in accord with the Decrees of Vatican Council II

By
REV. A. M. ROGUET, O.P.

Translated by
Rev. Walter van de Putte, C.S.Sp.

CATHOLIC BOOK PUBLISHING CO.
NEW YORK

This book was originally published in French under the title *La Messe d'aujourd'hui: Table Ouverte* by Desclée Co., Paris-Journal

NIHIL OBSTAT: Daniel V. Flynn, J.C.D.

Censor Librorum

IMPRIMATUR: Joseph P. O'Brien, S.T.D.

Vicar General, Archdiocese of New York

January 25, 1970

The nihil obstat and imprimatur are official declarations that a book or pamphlet is free of doctrinal or moral error. No implication is contained therein that those who have granted the nihil obstat and imprimatur agree with the contents, opinions or statements expressed.

ISBN 0-899-42130-x

(T-130)

TABLE OF CONTENTS

FOREWORD

*(Not indispensable for those
who were born after 1954)*

Our intention in writing this non-ponderous book is to explain to Christians, or even to curious unbelievers, what is the meaning of the so-called New Mass or the Mass of *today*.

By *today* we mean the period that has witnessed the restoration which was demanded by Vatican Council II.

In 1951 we wrote a similar book in the same simple style, but then we had to make frequent references to history because the Mass of that time presented itself as a legacy of the past. The reason for this was not the fact that the Mass as then celebrated was instituted by Jesus Christ on the eve of His Death: for the same is also true of the Mass of *today*; otherwise it would no longer be what we call "the Mass."

The reason was that the Mass of that time showed the marks of ecclesiastical institutions and of cultural forms. This made it necessary to know and recognize such features, if we wanted to understand things properly. That was still the situation in the first half of the present century.

Now, according to the *Constitution on the Sacred Liturgy* of Vatican Council II, if the Mass "Liturgy is made up of immutable elements divinely instituted" there are also elements

> subject to change. The latter not only may but ought to be changed with the passage of time if they have suffered from the intrusion of anything out of harmony with the inner nature of the Liturgy or have become unsuited to it.

In this restoration, both texts and rites should be drawn up so that they express more clearly the holy things which they signify. Christian people, as far as possible, should be enabled to understand them with ease and to take part in them fully, actively, and as befits a community (art. 21).[1]

[That is why] the rites should be distinguished by a noble simplicity; they should be short, clear, and unencumbered by useless repetitions; they should be within the people's powers of comprehension, and normally should not require much explanation (art. 34).

These principles apply, of course, to the Mass which is the heart of the whole Liturgy:

The rite of the Mass is to be revised in such a way that the intrinsic nature and purpose of its several parts, as also the connection between them, can be more clearly manifested, and that devout and active participation by the faithful can be more easily accomplished.

For this purpose the rites are to be simplified, while due care is taken to preserve their substance. Elements which, with the passage of time, came to be duplicated, or were added with but little advantage, are now to be discarded; other elements which have suffered injury through accidents of history are now to be restored to the vigor which they had in the days of the holy Fathers, as may seem useful or necessary (art. 50).

This revision of the Mass with respect to essentials has now been realized. (See no. 46, p. 185: *"Will the Mass undergo further changes?"*) We can, therefore, dispense ourselves from all retrospection and present the Mass as it is, leaving out references to the past with respect to things that have become useless. Surely it serves no good purpose to recall rites that have disappeared.

---

[1] The official translation of the Latin word *instauratio* reads "restoration"; it would be more correct to say "renovation," for there is no question of returning to the past because of a slavish love of all that is ancient. If such were the intention of the Conciliar text, it would use the term *restauratio*.

Revision of Mass Now accomplished

The readers who have known the Mass before 1964 [2] will pardon us if we do not justify the abolition or the change of prayers and gestures they have long known and loved. Comparisons of this sort would be unpleasant especially for younger Christians who have never known, for example, the recitation of the *Iudica me* ("Judge me, O Lord") at the foot of the altar, nor the "Last Gospel." The Mass of *today* must find its explanation in itself and not with reference to rites that have now been bypassed.

But, you may say, if its reform is done properly and the rites are "transparent," if they have a natural interconnection, what is the use of explanations? The *Constitution on the Sacred Liturgy* says explicitly that there will be no need for numerous explanations so that people might be able to understand them." Does this mean that this book is useless?

Need for Initiation, Not Explanation

We do *not* think so. First of all it will not give *numerous* explanations. Formerly it was necessary to recall numerous historical and archeological data to make rites comprehensible, but these, I repeat, we no longer need.

Secondly, this book will not give "explanations"; the Mass is not a Code that needs deciphering nor a theorem that demands demonstration. What is needed is *initiation*. The Mass is a *Mystery*, and a *Mystery* that presents itself to us in a ritual and *symbolic* clothing. A person may be most intelligent, have a strong faith, and the Mass celebration might be very well ordered, and yet such a believer could remain at the surface of the signs.

---

[2] The first revision of the liturgy of the Mass was promulgated by the *Instruction for the Proper Implementation of the Constitution on the Sacred Liturgy* of September 26, 1964. The faithful who were ten years old at that time, have, therefore, no remembrance of the condition of the Mass before that time, as it had been unchangeably fixed since the Middle Ages, and especially since the institution of the Sacred Congregation of Rites in 1588.

It is not our intention to present the reader with an abstract theology of the Mass which would give the key to these signs. We prefer to proceed in an inverse way. We shall look successively at the signs. We shall try to understand them in themselves and in their concatenation, so that the reader may be able to reach the thing signified, that is, the Mystery, by way of the sign.

This, at least, is the method recommended by the *Instruction on the Eucharistic Mystery* (art. 15), prepared by the "Consilium for the Implementation of the Constitution on the Sacred Liturgy," promulgated on May 25, 1967, by the Sacred Congregation of Rites:

> The Catechesis . . . should take as its starting point . . . the rites and prayers which are part of the Celebration. It should clarify their meaning, especially that of the great Eucharistic Prayer, and lead the people to a *profound understanding of the Mystery which those rites signify and accomplish.*

We feel certain that what the reader wants is the successive presentation of the rites of the Mass, for this is the way that is the most normal and also most clear. It is true, however, that this method involves the danger of suggesting that the Mass is an arbitrary series of detached rites. This fault we shall do our best to avoid.

With this in mind we shall, first of all, present the rites not only in their succession, but in their concatenation, showing their interconnection. Finally and above all, we shall try, for each in turn, to lead the reader "to a profound understanding of the Mystery which these rites signify and accomplish."

This Mystery is unique in its superabundant richness. The Mass constitutes a unity! We believe that in this way we shall have tried to give a true theology of the Mass to the reader. Not, we repeat, an abstract and *a priori* theology! But an inductive one, starting from particular facts—a theology that is liturgical and is also living.

I
PRELIMINARIES

1. I AM GOING TO CHURCH. . . .

It is Sunday, the Lord's Day. I am going to Mass. Therefore I am going to church.

Why "to church"? Could I not just as well, and even better, honor God by a personal, recollected, prayer? I should then be putting into practice what our Lord prescribed in the Sermon on the Mount: "When you pray, go into your room, and, closing your door, pray to your Father in secret; and your Father, Who sees in secret, will reward you" (Mt 6, 6).

It is certain that such a prayer—a prayer of petition, adoration, thanksgiving, or of simple attention to the presence of God—is absolutely indispensable to my life of faith. Without it I am not a friend of God, and my being a Christian has nothing then that is interior—it is not a life but a series of practices. I can exercise this living, profound prayer anywhere, in my room, on the street, on a bus or airplane, and in church, when it is silent, when there is no crowd taking part in a service.

That is true. Nevertheless, this way of praying is not enough. I am not an isolated individual, "an island," a pure spirit. Christians have been redeemed *in a body*, and this is so in a twofold meaning of the word. They have been redeemed in their bodies, and not only in their souls. And by the very fact that they have a body they have a social life. They form *a Body* with their fellowmen and still more with their Christian brethren. Jesus has not merely saved individuals. He has also, or rather first, engendered a Church, an assembly, the "People of God," which is also *His Body*. It is here that individuals must find all their personal development.

This notion of "People of God" already played a considerable role in the Old Testament. The People of God had been constituted, gathered, sanctified, consecrated to Him as a bride is united to her husband—by the Covenant, particularly the one sealed by Moses after the liberating crossing of the sea, on Mount Sinai (Ex 24, 1-8).

But the prophets announced a new Covenant for the future (Jer 31, 31) which was infinitely more intimate, more profound, and more holy. This is the Covenant Jesus came to realize by His Blood (Mk 22, 20), "He is mediator of a new Covenant, that whereas a death has taken place for redemption from the transgressions committed under the former Covenant, they who have been called may receive eternal inheritance according to the promise" (Heb 9, 15).

It is this new Covenant, this union of God with the whole people, which we are called to celebrate, to deepen, to make more close, and how could we do this in solitude? It can be achieved only with the People of God, *with the whole Church.* Hence, it should be done *in church,* in the edifice that got its name from the fact that the Church, the assembly of the believers, comes together there, being at the same time enveloped and signified by the edifice.

2. ON SUNDAY

But why precisely on Sunday? God is eternal. For Him all days have equal value! This is true, but I am not outside time as God is. Neither do my Christian brethren live outside time. If we wish to make sure we shall meet, there must be a rendezvous, a fixed day for the gathering.

Why Sunday? Was the new Covenant not sealed in Christ's Blood on Calvary, on Good Friday? It is true too that He offered that Blood, under the aspect of wine, with "the cup of the new Covenant in His Blood"; but this took place on Holy Thursday, at the Last Supper. So why renew this rite on Sunday?

We do indeed repeat at Mass what Jesus did for the first time on Holy Thursday. But we should not content ourselves with repeating a rite however venerable that rite might be. By celebrating it we certainly believe we are accomplishing the Mystery which was contained in that rite. This Mystery is the Mystery of His Sacrifice and of our salvation. And the Sacrifice is not completed with the immolation of the Victim. Our salvation is not obtained by the mere fact that Christ has died. It is necessary that the immolation end in union with God, in holiness, to the glory of the humiliated Victim that was put to death for sin. This means that the Sacrifice of Christ comprises the Mystery of His Death and His Resurrection.

The Resurrection is not just a joyful epilogue that serves to wipe out the painful memory of a most cruel death. It is its end and finale. Death is only a passage; the Resurrection is its term and its purpose. We go to Mass on Sunday because we celebrate the Christ Who died centuries ago but Who, having risen, is still today the Risen One.

It is on "the first day of the week" that Jesus inaugurated His life as the Risen Savior, with His disciples, by appearing to them on the evening of Easter. He appeared to them a second time eight days later. That "first day of the week" has become His Day, the Day of the Lord (Dominica dies). It is Jesus Himself Who has instituted His Day, not by way of a precept but by way of a fact.

Christians, by assembling every Sunday to celebrate the Paschal Mystery, recall and renew what is essential in their faith and the source-principle of their salvation: "If you confess with your mouth that Jesus is the Lord, and believe in your heart that God has raised Him from the dead, you shall be saved" (Rm 10, 9). But by participating in the Mass, I am doing more than professing by word of mouth and believing in my heart that Jesus has risen. I proclaim it actively, existentially, by celebrating the Mystery in which He lives the very Act of His sacrifice, of His Death-and-Resurrection.

The Church, for some time now, has given permission to Christians to comply with this fundamental law by partici-

pating in the Mass on Saturday evening. In doing so she is
not allowing them to celebrate the Day of the Lord on another day. She is merely admitting, in line with the whole
Jewish tradition to which the Liturgy has remained faithful,
that the Day of the Lord begins on the evening of Saturday. [1]

Moreover, the experience of this anticipation shows that
the Christian assembly is more peaceful and recollected at
that time than on Sunday morning. As for Mass on other
days, it too is a Pasch, an Easter, as is every Eucharist, but
it is so less eminently. The Paschal Eucharist is the one celebrated on the Day of the Lord, on Sunday.

3. I ENTER THE CHURCH

I enter the church a few minutes before the time for Mass.
This I do for myself, for God, and for my brethren.

For myself. To recollect myself, to put myself in the right
frame of mind before beginning to take part in the liturgical
Action. It is not a question of forgetting my daily life, my real
life, my cares and concerns. On the contrary, these are the
starting point of my prayer. I do not come to Mass to evade
them. Still more: they are the matter of my offering and of
my sacrifice. But I need to place an interval between secular
life and my entry into the Sacred, precisely so that my secular
life may fully enter into it.

For God. I do not present myself before an important per-
sonage in dirty clothes, when I am out of breath and am apt
to act in a disorderly fashion. Before entering into the Sacred
Action, before speaking officially to God, with my brethren,
I need a moment to put myself in His presence and silently
adore Him. The more time and care I take to get hold of myself, to get the right orientation, to renew my intention of
truly praying with all, the more fully and personally I shall
participate in this Community Action.

---

[1] Vespers, we may remark, the evening Office, of Saturday, is still
called "First Vespers of Sunday."

For my brethren. Nothing so greatly spoils the quality of a praying assembly as constant new arrivals, as stragglers who perhaps always come late for train and bus and seem to like to jump on moving vehicles. And latecomers then distract others by looking here and there for an empty seat while a prayer or solemn reading is in progress.

Of course, we cannot do away with this type of disorderly and negligent person. But I can make sure I do not become a straggler. And I can only hope that I shall not have to suffer from the zigzag course of those who are hunting for a place. What I ought to do is *not* to take the first empty seat I see near the door, leaving large zones near the altar more empty than a desert. All places belong to all, for in Jesus Christ there is neither Jew nor Greek, neither man nor woman, neither rich nor poor.

The only places reserved are those for the ministers of the altar and for members of the choir, readers, commentators. So I place myself where I shall best be able to participate in the service, that is, where I shall see better and hear better and do my part from the time of my arrival to the formation of an at first restricted but already compact assembly.

Gradually the assembly is forming around me. In it are all sorts of people; they have come from every corner of the parish and belong to all categories. There are also strangers; people do travel nowadays! Such a mixture ought not to displease me. It might be pleasant to participate in the Mass with people who have the same origin, the same culture, the same social rank, the same religious fervor (or lukewarmness?). But the Church is neither a club nor a confraternity; it is like a "big sheet" like the one Peter saw "let down from heaven" and which was filled with all sorts of animals and wild beasts—everything possible that could walk, crawl or fly (Acts 10, 11; 11, 6) like the Ark of Noah.

If, from time to time, I like to celebrate the Eucharist with a restricted and homogeneous group of brethren who have the same concerns, perhaps the same professional occupations or the same apostolic views as myself, I ought, on Sunday, to do my best to find my Lord again in a motley assembly that is made up of the rich and the poor, of old breed and new breed, of professors and workmen, of old people and children; an assembly that is not only a portion but an image and as it were the sacrament of the universal Church, which is spread all over the world, a sign and a leaven of salvation of all mankind.

4. DO I NEED MY BOOK?

In principle, no. We do not go to the theatre, unless we are foreigners, in order to follow the text of the play in a book. Likewise at a concert, we do not read the score unless we are expert musicians or critics and desire to verify the proper execution of the music. We look and we listen; that is all.

The Mass is also a spectacle and an audition, even if it is much more than that. It is proper, and it suffices, to look and listen. Perhaps the habits created by a civilization of the Press, of the printed word, prompt us to read. But the age of radio, records, movies and television has taught us to use our eyes for other things than reading, and to use our ears for listening, which is quite different from passive hearing.

A book does not seem to be needed, since the Mass is said, almost completely, in an intelligible voice and in our own language. The use of a book might cause annoyance and distraction. Because of the liberty now permitted by the present Liturgy, we are not always able to know ahead of time which prayer, which Readings, which Eucharistic Prayer the priest will choose; it takes time to find them in our book, and the Prayer or Reading is over or already far gone and we have not heard anything!

It is true that the priest says some prayers in a low voice, but they have only a secondary importance and are not meant for the assembly. Let us use this time profitably by freely praying in silence.

The Mass has other moments of silence: at the beginning of the Penitential Rite, before the first Prayer, after the Communion, after certain Readings. Are my mind and heart so empty that I have to fill in such silences with readings? They are not holes that have to be filled in. They are breathing spells which I must learn to use profitably in order to make the prayer in common more personal.

Needed Both at Church and at Home

However, the above is true only in ideal situations. In reality, the church may have poor acoustics, the priest or reader may not be an expert in proper pronunciation, and I may not be blest with good hearing. . . . A book then becomes a necessary remedy, like crutches for a limping man, or glasses for a shortsighted person.

But all this does not mean that I shall not own a Missal. A Mass Book will no doubt be divided once more in the traditional way of Christian antiquity; the "Sacramentary" or Book of the Prayers of the Priest, and the "Lectionary." They, especially the second one, will be rather important books but hard to bring along. But I shall have them at home.

The Prayers and the scriptural Readings, which henceforth will have great diversity, cannot be fully assimilated at only one hearing, because of their spiritual density and also, in the case of the Readings, because of the importance of their context. On that account, it will be necessary to read them ahead of time, perhaps to read them again afterward and to meditate upon them.

I must own and use "Mass Books" outside the Celebration, a Celebration that I should not change into a school exercise, but in which I must participate freely and joyfully. Such books will be my constant companions and guides at home; in them I shall find the privileged school for my personal participation; they will be irreplaceable instruments of religious culture and the exercise of mental prayer.

5. THE PLACES OF THE CELEBRATION

When I was a child and was taken to the circus or to the theater, nothing in the world could make me want to get there when the show was already in progress or even to come "just in time." Surely the most beautiful moments were those minutes of waiting, of expectancy, before an empty arena or a lowered curtain; for these seemed already to vibrate and soon they would be flooded with light and what marvels would then be revealed!

I hope no one will be shocked by my recalling such secular experiences in the present context. The Mass can certainly not be compared to a show, which is usually full of happenings and leads to an unexpected finale. And yet when we come to church a little ahead of time, when the faithful are already gathering but the sanctuary is still waiting for the ministers, we can already relish the Mystery which will be enacted. For the edifice itself, the arrangements in the church, make us anticipate what will soon be celebrated.

If the sacred edifice is well adapted to its function (and this is not always the case for reasons of art and history, if not through routine), it seems to preserve the imprint of the Action that has taken place in it. And we could say just as well (for it is a question here of reciprocal causes and effects): it announces the Celebration which will shape itself in line with that house of the Lord.

Nave and Sanctuary

Together with the other faithful I am in the "nave" or vessel, in which the People of God come together. It is at the same time a sacred people and a people of equals, for it is born of one same Baptism. All the members of this People are equal in the sense that no account is taken of diversities of rank, culture, nationality, or race. Modern architecture permits the whole people to gather without being broken up into compartments of first or second or third class. The People, however, is also "sacred," that is, polarized, unified by the unique Divine Mystery which is to be accomplished not only before but also for and through this People.

Hence, the nave is not a closed hall. It is rather a vessel that is on a cruise fully directed to a port or goal that enters infinitude. The nave is not simply ending at the sanctuary; it opens toward it; it is connected with it, even if a variety of barriers still remains. In older churches we will find chancels, railings. Today a good number of churches still have steps leading into the sanctuary and the sanctuary may have a higher or a lower vault than the nave, and a more glorious light may illumine it and there is more space that is left free.

In this sanctuary it is the altar that holds the primary rank. A table, indeed, but one that deserves the name "Holy Table." It is not a very large table for it is merely called to bear the Eucharistic gifts and a Book. For the present, in any case, it is still empty. It will serve only for the Eucharistic Action, an Action that may not be performed elsewhere. The Cross which dominates it serves to remind us that this Table is the place of a sacrifice. The lighted candles announce that it will be the celebration of a living sacrifice whose Victim is a glorious Victim.

Logically, the altar is turned toward the assembly; is it not from there that the priest will call the people to render thanks (Eucharist)? If, however, the altar faces the opposite way, it can then be said that the priest merely leads the people on their march heaven-ward, as a shepherd advances at the head of the flock (Jn 10, 4).

Altar, Ambo, Presidential Seat

In the sanctuary there is another table, even if it does not look like one. It is the Table of the Word, called "ambo," which comes from a Greek verb signifying "to ascend": for it is a platform to which the reader or lector ascends so as to be seen and heard by all (Neh 8, 4-5). It is also from there that the priest can make his comments and apply the Word of

God in a homily. Finally, it is from there that the priest or the deacon can express the intentions of the Universal Prayer (prayer of the faithful). If it is necessary to address the people for other things such as announcements, admonitions, it is proper to do it from another place which is purely functional, and not from the sacred place.

There is a third place which is necessary for the Celebration, and which is quite distinct from the two others; this is the place of "the presidency." This term seems pompous; it recalls nevertheless that the priest is not a "solitary," is not the sole actor in the Celebration; for the Celebration belongs to the whole people. He is only the "one who presides," the president, and is similar to the conductor of an orchestra.

The place of the presidency must be situated in the sanctuary in such a way that the one who presides can well see the people, and can be seen and heard by the people, and remains in communication with it. In basilicas of Rome or Africa, in the first centuries, the seat of the bishop was in the back, under the half- cupola of the *absis* or apse which broadcast his voice. In many churches today, this place would be too far off. The proper place for the one who presides should be determined according to the structure of the edifice, and thus it is impossible to give a universal rule in this regard.

It is at this place of the presidency that the priest greets the people, fulfills the Penitential Rite (general confession of sins), says the first (and often the last) Oration; it is there that he listens to the Word of God proclaimed by others; it is there that he opens and closes the Universal Prayer if the intentions are expressed by another from the ambo; it is there that he breaks up the assembly by the blessing and the final dismissal.

We have enumerated these three places of the Celebration in an order of decreasing importance. They are occupied in an inverse order in the course of the Celebration. The celebrant sits at the place of the presidency for the Introductory Rites and to listen to the Word of God. He ascends the ambo to proclaim and interpret this Word. He finally goes up to the altar to prepare the gifts, then for the Eucharistic Prayer and for the Communion.

6. PRESENCES OF CHRIST

If we were to imagine that the Mass has for its purpose to make Christ present in a purely physical and static way in our churches of stone, like a jewel in a ring, we would be doomed to understand nothing about the Eucharistic Mystery, and this, first of all, because we would be committing a grave error with respect to the mystery of the Church.

Christ's Presence with His Church

Christ is always with His Church. He promised this to His Apostles as He was ready to withdraw His visible presence: "Behold, I am with you all days, even unto the consummation of the world" (His last words in St. Matthew's Gospel: 28, 20). "I will not leave you orphans" (Jn 14, 18): and in fact He has sent us His Spirit, Who remains in us. And the Father grants us that Christ dwells in our hearts "through [our] faith" (Eph 3, 17).

However precious and comforting may be this assistance, this presence, this indwelling of Christ, it is spiritual, absolutely invisible. We have a sensible and social nature and it demands something different: the presence of Christ to His Church through visible and active signs. This is the first reason for the existence of the Liturgy, and hence of the Mass which is its center (so much so that the the Eastern Christians use the term "Liturgy" to designate what we call the Mass).

The Liturgy has a second reason for existence which is closely connected with the first, namely, to make us use signs, given by God, to make us send up to God, in a visible and social way, our supplications, our adoration, our acts of thanksgiving.

Christ's Presence in the Liturgy

Hence, in the Liturgy Christ is present to His Church in a most special way, which no private or even common non-liturgical prayer even when most fervent can replace. He is thus present to His Church in four ways.

Let us note that these are four modes of *real* presence, a presence which is perfectly objective, which does not depend, as for instance in private prayer, on the good disposition or even on the state of grace of the individuals who are present. Two of those modes are fulfilled in every liturgical Celebration, for example, in the celebration of the Word of God, and in that of the Divine Office, notably in Lauds and Vespers the Church's official morning and evening prayers.

Christ "is always present in a body of the faithful gathered in His name" (cf. Mt 18, 20). This He has promised and we can somewhat understand that great mystery; for Baptism has made us members of Christ, each one for our part; hence when we are together, we really form the sacramental Body of Christ (cf. 1 Cor 6, 15; 12, 27).

Christ "is present too in His Word, for it is He Who speaks when the Scriptures are read in the Church." This presence is particularly active when the Church is not only "assembled in His name" but when it prays and when it sings the Psalms, for these are part of the Holy Scripture and it is Christ Himself Who then speaks and prays by the mouth of His faithful.

The other two modes of Christ's presence are realized only in the Eucharistic Celebration. First in the priest. Christ is already present in him because he presides over and recapitulates the assembly of the baptized who are the Body of Christ. But Christ is present in the priest in virtue of another title and a higher one, when he presides over the faithful at the Eucharist. For the priest offers the Eucharist in the name of, and even as acting in the person of, Christ; so much so that he then says: "This is My Body delivered for you." And it is well known that the body about which he says that it is "My Body" is in reality the Body of Christ.

By this fact then the Eucharist realizes one last presence of Christ, under the appearances of bread and wine which *are* the Body and Blood of Christ. But this presence is not merely real as are also those mentioned above. "In this Sacrament Christ is present in a unique way, whole and entire, God and Man, substantially and permanently."

Hence, in the Eucharistic Celebration Christ is present in an active way that is absolutely special: as Priest and Victim, offering Himself in a sacrifice of Covenant and thanksgiving, recapitulating and appropriating His whole People to make this People in turn priest and victim of the unique Sacrifice.

This presence is active, dynamic, but not on that account transitory. It is a "substantial and permanent" presence. Hence, when the sacrifice is over, when Communion has been distributed, the Hosts that remain continue to realize Christ's presence among us. That is why they are preserved in the tabernacle from which they can be taken to give Communion outside of Mass, especially to the sick and as viaticum to the dying.

It is proper, therefore, for the faithful to pay visits and adore Christ particularly present in the permanent Eucharist, all the while not forgetting that those Hosts have been consecrated at Mass, in the Paschal Sacrifice, and that they are destined to be received in a holy communion, enabling the recipients to participate in the Paschal Mystery for which they have received the power in Baptism.

But this explains also why such a permanent presence takes "second" place, which by no means makes it secondary and unimportant. It is a derived presence with respect to the active presences that are realized in the Eucharistic Action.

This is why it is proper for the Blessed Sacrament to be kept in a special chapel that is adorned as it deserves and helps to create an atmosphere of recollection, instead of being placed on the altar where Mass is celebrated. For in the latter situation, we invert the order of the presences of Christ which we have described above. When the Blessed Sacrament is already on the altar of sacrifice, the Eucharistic Presence which is supreme, "incomparable," precedes the presences which in reality come before it namely: Christ's presence in the assembly, in the Word, in the priest, and then in the Sacrifice. [2]

7. THE PRIESTHOOD OF THE BAPTIZED AND ACTIVE PARTICIPATION

Who celebrates Mass? We do not hesitate to say that it is the Christian assembly. The verb *celebrare* (to celebrate) is connected, after all, with the adjective *celeber* which, in Latin means populous. To "celebrate" is the Action of the Christian People because this people is, in virtue of its Baptism, a priestly people, a holy and consecrated people, which therefore is able to offer the sacrifice, as priest, and at the same time, to be offered with Him, as victim.

Of course, this assembly, in order really to offer the Eucharist, must be presided over by a priest. But, precisely, the latter is only a president: the whole of Christian antiquity uses

[2] This doctrine of the presence of Christ was already sketched in the Encyclical *Mediator Dei,* on the Liturgy, by Pope Pius XII. It was more fully expressed in the *Constitution on the Sacred Liturgy,* art. 7 (and in art. 33 with respect to Christ's active presence in the Word). Since then it has been more methodically presented in the *Instruction on the Eucharistic Mystery,* art. 9. All the texts quoted above are taken from this article. Article 55 of the same *Instruction* concludes from it that it is proper not to keep the Blessed Sacrament on the altar where Mass is celebrated. Finally, the Encyclical of Paul VI, *Mysterium Fidei,* gives an ample explanation of the diverse modes of Christ's presence in His Church, nos. 35-38 . Here it is said that the real presence under the Eucharistic species is called "real" not in an exclusive way as if the other presences were not "real," but it is real par excellence, because it is *substantial* and by it Christ, God and Man, makes Himself wholly present" (no. 39), quoted in *Instruction on the Eucharistic Mystery,* no. 9 . The relation of the Eucharistic adoration to the Mass and to the Paschal Mystery is stressed in the latter *Instruction,* no. 50.

this word to designate his function; it never uses the term "celebrant" which would imply a sort of monopoly. The priest is for the assembly, is at its service. It is only with the assembly, whether present or not, that he can offer. This is why he always speaks in the plural: "We offer, we give thanks, we pray."

It can happen that a priest consecrates the Eucharist without the visible presence of an assembly, but the latter must be represented at least by a server or one who makes the responses. It may even happen in cases of extreme necessity that a priest celebrates absolutely alone. He will, nevertheless, continue to speak in the plural, precisely because, as priest, he represents and recapitulates the whole assembly, speaks in the name of the whole people, although the people seems to be absent. Here it is the exception that confirms the rule: the isolated priest represents the people because, normally, he celebrates only with the people and for the people. A Church without a people, reduced to a simple priestly caste, is inconceivable. The Church is the People of God.

But by what title is the priest the representative of the people? Not in the sense that he is its delegate, its deputy. The priestly power is not a reality that is first diffused in the people which then by the will of the people is concentrated and crystallized in the priest. The priest represents the people only because first he represents Christ, the unique Priest. God calls a person to the ministerial priesthood through the voice of the bishop who appoints him for the service of the people. It is because he takes the place of Christ, Who is the Head of the people and the Source of all priesthood, that the priest represents the people.

In contrast with the people, which represents Christ collectively, the priest represents Christ personally. This is why the priest alone can consecrate the bread and wine, when he says, or rather when Christ says through his lips: "This is My Body, which will be given up for you. This is the cup of My Blood. . . ." In the other sacraments the priest acts personally, as a minister, an instrument, who says: "I baptize, I absolve, I confirm."

When it concerns the Eucharist, he effaces himself, as it were, before Christ Who acts through him. In this respect, his ministerial priesthood (that is, one in the service of the People of God) differs in nature from the common priesthood of the baptized. [3] But he himself is a baptized person. Hence, though the priest alone can consecrate, he offers and receives Communion like the people, for and with it.

How the Faithful Participate at Mass

Since Christ is the only true priest, Who, "by one offering has perfected forever those who are sanctified" (Heb 10, 14), the ministerial priest and the people in the Eucharist are merely *participating*. This term, so frequently used nowadays, has a very precise meaning. It signifies "to take part in," "to exercise a part." We may compare it to musicians who execute a portion of a score in a symphony. The ministerial priest seen by the faithful is at the same time a soloist and the director of the orchestra, of the symphony.

How do the faithful play their part, their role? First by faith and by charity. They are not satisfied with a mere assistance at the Mystery like foreign spectators. They adhere to it, they enter into it with their whole being. They offer by a spiritual activity that can be expressed externally by a concrete offering, by bringing gifts to the altar or simply by contributing to the collection, but also by their attentive presence, their active silence, their attitudes that harmonize with the phases of the Action, by their respon-

---

[3] This doctrine of the common priesthood of the baptized and of the ministerial priesthood of the priest is explained in the *Constitution on the Sacred Liturgy*, art. 7. 14. 26. 27. 30. 33; in the *Constitution on the Church*, art. 10 and 11. 31-36; in the *Decree on the Ministry and Life of Priests*, art. 5 and 6. For the question of the priest holding the place of the whole Church, of the whole People, cf. St. Thomas, *Summa Theologica*, Part III, Qu. 80, art. 12, ans. 3; Qu. 82, art. 6.

ses to the dialogue begun by the priest, by their acclamations and their chants.

Finally and above all they participate most actively and most profoundly, by receiving Holy Communion. For *"communicare"* (to communicate) here means not merely to "receive" the Body and Blood of Christ, at the end of an Action which they might have witnessed in a passive way. It consists in "taking" the Body and the Blood of Christ to which the faithful have contributed by offering it together with the priest, while they offer themselves with him.

All this is what is meant by the "active participation" so often demanded from the faithful by the Council's *Constitution on the Sacred Liturgy*. And it does not consist in acting in any sort of way and at every moment, but in playing their true role, according to their particular place in the priestly People of God.

8. THE DEACON

When reading what we have just explained we might come to believe that the celebration of Mass admits of only two actors: the people and the priest who presides over the people, represents and recapitulates it, and consecrates the Body and Blood of Christ for it. This indeed is frequently the view of the Mass held by many of the faithful because of the way it is in fact most frequently celebrated: the people are in the nave, and the priest is alone in the sanctuary although he may be assisted more or less by servers.

In a Mass that is truly communitarian, this is not so. The priest and the assembly are bound together by *ministers*. Although the priest is a minister of God and of the People of God, the term "minister" is mostly used to designate those who exercise functions that are lower than the function of the priest.

There is, first of all, the deacon. He is a privileged minister; though he does not have the power to consecrate the Eucharist (nor can he absolve, anoint the sick, and administer confirmation through delegation received from the Bishop), he is a member of the clergy, he belongs to the hierarchy. And the hierarchy has authority in sacred things. Moreover, he is "minister" par excellence for his original Greek name, *diakonos,* means servant and has been translated by the Latin term *minister* which sounds the same in English. This term is frequently used in the Gospel, for example, when Jesus says that the "Son of Man has not come to be served but to serve" (Mt 20, 28 and parallels).

In the West, for many centuries, the diaconate has been only a step toward the priesthood. Vatican Council II has reestablished a permanent diaconate as it existed in ancient times, and this Order may be conferred upon married men *(Constitution on the Church,* art. 29).

At Mass, the deacon assists the priest. [4] He can help in giving directions and admonitions for the proper participation of the faithful. It is his function to read the Gospel. The priest may also entrust him with preaching. The deacon announces the intentions of the Universal Prayer (often called Prayer of the Faithful). He helps the priest in distributing Communion, especially in presenting the chalice to the communicants when this is permitted. Finally, he dismisses the assembly which the presiding priest has just blessed.

The "Mass with a deacon," that is, when the priest is assisted by a deacon, is, then, an excellent realization of the Eucharistic Liturgy; it makes good use of two grades in the Church hierarchy, causing them to exercise the functions that are proper to them, and no others:

> In liturgical Celebrations each person, minister or lay-
> man, who has an office to perform, should do all of, but

[4] Outside of Mass, the functions of the deacon are very numerous. He can prepare for, and administer Baptism, doing the latter in the solemn form. He can bless marriages; can bring viaticum to the dying; preach, administer certain sacramentals (blessings), preside at funerals *(Ibid.).*

only, those parts which pertain to his office by the nature
of the rite and the principles of the Liturgy *(Constitution
on the Sacred Liturgy*, art. 28).

This prescription, which at first sight seems insignificant,
will prove to be one of the most fruitful for the renewal of
the Liturgy. It reestablishes, the "symphonic" character of an
Action in which every individual, "minister *or faithful"—*
as is most important to note—fulfills the participation that
belongs to him. Too long had people seen a priest doing and
saying everything, in the presence of ministers who sometimes seemed to be present purely for decorative effect, and
a people that was inert.

9. THE OTHER MINISTERS

Whether there is a deacon or not, other subordinate functions are fulfilled by lay people. These in technical liturgical
language are called *ministrantes* (servers) rather than *minis-
tri* (ministers). Although they have not received any ordination, they are not walkers-on; they are not lay persons who
merely "render service" helping the clergy for example in
organizing a charity bazaar. On the contrary, there they
fulfill a true liturgical ministry and thus exercise their baptismal priesthood in a sort of specialized way. We can without scruple call them ministers.

They can be considered from two aspects: Since they are
members of the laity we may look upon them as delegates
of the people in relation to the priest. But we may also consider them emissaries of the priest to the people because
they are given ministerial functions. In fact, they have both
these roles and, whatever their proper tasks may be, their
activity has the advantage of establishing a go-between, a
living communication between the nave and the sanctuary.

Some of these ministers can exercise functions which come
very close to those pertaining to the deacon. First of all,
there are those which concern the proclamation of the Word.

As lectors (readers) they can ascend to the ambo to read from the Scriptures, with the exception of the Gospel which must be read by the priest if no deacon is available. At the ambo they may also read the intentions of the Universal Prayer. Finally, but in a place outside the ambo, they may give monitions, that is they can act as "commentators." But this role which was important when it was necessary to make the laity participate in the Liturgy when it was still in Latin, no longer has reason for existence. If the Mass on rare occasions still needs brief monitions, they belong rather to the priest who presides at the Celebration.

Such ministers may also supply for the deacon, with respect to the Eucharist, properly so-called, by assisting the priest at the altar, bringing him the gifts of the faithful, and even—in certain cases, and with the necessary permission —helping in the administration of Communion.

It is also part of the liturgical ministry of the Word of God when such persons chant the verses of the Psalm that is part of the Introit or Entrance Song, as also the one that follows the first Reading, and the one that accompanies the procession at Communion. But this can also be done by the choir; such a choir is not a mere group of artists charged with embellishing the Celebration, and charming or distracting the faithful. The "choir" here means a group of the faithful who, no doubt, are expected to be relatively competent musically speaking, but they too exercise a true liturgical function either in prompting or sustaining the chant of the faithful, or in singing for them pieces that are more difficult but that will contribute to the beauty of worship and to producing an atmosphere of recollection and contemplation.

Finally, the faithful who act as ushers, help in the organization of processions, who take up the collection, distribute booklets and the weekly sheet of announcements, also exercise a true liturgical function, for they contribute to a smoother active participation on the part of all.

10. CONCELEBRATION

Sometimes, in your parish, in a seminary or religious community, especially where many priests come together, you assist at a Mass that is celebrated by many priests who together pronounce the words of Consecration. This we call Concelebration. What is the meaning of this rite?

Let me recall a personal memory. When I was a young priest, we were assembled for the eminently personal and silent exercise called meditation or mental prayer. When the moment had come for the celebration of Masses then called "private," we proceeded to small separate altars, sometimes located in a basement. It took me a long time to see how illogical it was to practice in common so private and secret a prayer as meditation and then to separate and celebrate individually the Sacrifice of Unity. The impression given by those separate Masses was that of a sign of division, or at least of multiplicity. Now concelebration is a corrective for that bad logic.

Certainly, it is a good thing and will always be necessary to celebrate many Masses. It would be impossible for many churches in the city or in the country to house all the faithful at one time for one Mass. The varieties of occupations of the faithful and the rhythms of life demand a great diversity of hours for Masses if it is desired to really minister to the faithful as priests are called to do.

Strengthens Unity of Priesthood

But in case there are no such needs and several priests are to do so, why not perform the Sacred Action together, so as to express and strengthen the unity of their priesthood? This in fact is the true reason for concelebration. If, in addition, concelebration solves certain practical problems in the life of priests, this is only a secondary reason. [5]

And if concelebration adds solemnity to that Sacred Function, this is not *the* purpose that was predominant. We must recognize, nevertheless, that a priestly or episcopal ordination is particularly beautiful and meaningful when the Holy Sacrifice is concelebrated not only by the bishop with his new priest(s) or his new colleague, but also with the priests who have contributed to direct a vocation, with those in whose apostolate the new bishop has had a share, and with those who henceforth will have him as their father and inspiring leader.

Hence the faithful ought not to imagine that concelebration is a purely clerical matter which does not concern them. The Mystery of the Church is a Mystery of Unity, and this the Mass represents, exercises, and vivifies. It is the Mystery of Unity of all in Christ. One of its aspects, perhaps one of its foundations, is the mystery of unity of all priests in the Unique Priest.

The faithful who share in this priesthood in a subordinate way, also participate in concelebration. When they participate in the most "humble," most "ordinary" Mass, they concelebrate within the limits of the powers proper to them in virtue of Baptism. Hence, they must not be surprised to see priests doing the same thing, according to their rank. Better still, by participating actively in the concelebration of their priests, the faithful can acquire a more vivid sense of the unity of the Church, of her priesthood and of her sacrifice. [6]

---

[5] There is, for instance, a touching realization achieved by concelebration when it permits priests who are blind or seriously ill and unable to say Mass (except possibly in an isolated spot and with ever the same formulary) to perform that Great Action so dear to every good priest (cf. *Rite of Concelebration,* nos. 140-155).

[6] "Concelebration of the Eucharist aptly demonstrates the unity of the sacrifice and of the priesthood. Moreover, whenever the faithful take an active part, the unity of the People of God is strikingly manifested, particularly if the bishop presides. Concelebration both sym-

Fundamentally, if some have been disconcerted by the practice of concelebration, it is because they had a somewhat false idea of the priesthood: they saw in the priest, personally, another Christ, a sort of sacred monarch, a man who possessed, as a personal privilege, the words that can consecrate as well as those that can absolve. It is good for all, priests as well the faithful, to realize concretely that one is not a priest for oneself nor for oneself alone, but as part of a team, the *presbyterium,* presided over by the bishop, in the service of the people, to represent the Unique Priest, Who is as unique when represented by several as when represented by one alone. This makes us understand that all Masses, in their inevitable multiplicity, are always but reflections, so to speak, of the unique Sacrifice of the Last Supper and the Cross.

11. SYNOPSIS

Before going on to examine the unfolding course of the Mass, we must have a look at its overall plan. For it is not an arbitrary collection of rites, so that, we could, for example, begin with the last part and end with the first. It is an organic Action that obediently follows one sole movement.

It comprises two great parts: the *Liturgy of the Word* and the *Liturgy of the Eucharist.* We shall, at the opportune time, see their internal relation, realizing that these two parts "form but one single act of worship" *(Constitution on the Sacred Liturgy,* art. 56).

1. The *Liturgy of the Word* is preceded by the *Introductory Rites.*

----

bolizes and strengthens the brotherly bond of the priesthood, because 'by virtue of the ordination to the priesthood which they have in common, all are bound together in an intimate brotherhood' " *(Instruction on the Eucharistic Mystery,* art. 47). The last sentence is a quotation from the *Decree on the Ministry and Life of Priests,* art. 8, on the unity of the *presbyterium,* the priestly team).

The Universal Prayer (Prayer of the Faithful) forms the transition from the Liturgy of the Word to the Liturgy of the Eucharist.

2. The *Liturgy of the Eucharist* comprises three phases:

a) the bringing of the gifts to the altar;

b) the Eucharistic Prayer properly so-called which constitutes the Offering and the Sacrifice;

c) the rites of Communion, that is, the participation in the Sacrifice. Finally, everything ends with the *Concluding Rites* and the Dismissal.

This simple enumeration already suffices to show that the diverse parts, if they follow one another, are in no way independent, like a variety of strangers standing in line to buy a ticket. Their multiplicity is no more a means of dispersion than that of the members and organs of a living body. When separated from one another they are anatomic debris. United they form one single body, animated by one and the same life.

In the Mass, this life has one summit, one center and one heart; it is the recalling and reiteration of the Action of Jesus at the Last Supper: at the same time an offering, a consecration, a sacrifice of reconciliation and covenant, and also a memorial. But this summit, and center, can neither be understood nor lived if it is isolated from the rest which prepares for it, completes and concludes it, which makes Christ's unique sacrifice the sacrifice of the Church, the Mystery of Faith.

II
INTRODUCTORY RITES AND PRAYERS

12. THE PRIEST'S GREETING TO THE ALTAR AND TO THE PEOPLE

The Mass begins with the entry of the priest into the sanctuary. Until then the faithful had more or less formed a group. It is the entry of the priest that transforms this aggregate of individuals into a holy, liturgical assembly, into one body which will organically celebrate the Sacrifice.

Hence, it is not simply to express their deference toward their presiding priest that the faithful rise as he enters. It is because they become aware at that moment of their unity, of their being assembled for the Sacred Action that is beginning. And if the priest plays the role of a catalyst inducing a new combination, it is surely not in virtue of his dignity or his personal superiority. It is because he renders Christ present (cf. above, no. 6: *Presences of Christ*, p. 19).

From the very beginning the priest will manifest his function which is that of connecting Christ and the people. That is why his first two movements consist in greeting the altar and greeting the people.

The Altar Represents Christ

He first greets the altar bowing before it, or makes a genuflection if the Sacred Species are kept in the tabernacle; he then kisses the altar table. For the altar represents Christ. Not of course in an active, dynamic, and real way, but only in a static manner, as a material object and a symbolic one. This representation of Christ by the altar has been explained by the fact that the altar is of stone and that Christ "is the stone," the rock which both protected and quenched the thirst of the Hebrews in the desert, [1] and secondly because He is the cornerstone of the edifice which is the Church. [2]

But, much more profoundly, Christ is the point of junction, the ladder or step between heaven and earth. [3] It is at the altar that mankind meets God through the Sacrifice; and Jesus is at the same time our sacrifice and the altar on which our gifts are presented so as to be acceptable to God, for "which is greater, the gift or the altar which sanctifies the gift?" (Mt 23, 18-20), so much so that, as St. Augustine tells us in defining the Sacrifice, "the Sacrifice unites us to God in a holy communion."

After the priest kisses the altar he may incense it. He then goes to the "place of the presidency."

When the singing or recitation of the Entrance Song is finished, the priest and the people make the sign of the Cross. The priest says: "In the name of the Father, and of the Son, and of the Holy Spirit." The people answer: "Amen." This is a formula frequently used by Christians, at the beginning of an action.

Hence, we might say that it is not only an invocation of the Blessed Trinity. It is also a reminder of our Baptism, for it was conferred "in the name" of the three Divine Persons, which means that it has consecrated us to their glory and introduced us into their intimate society. If we can celebrate the Mass with the priest, it is because we are baptized persons, incorporated in Christ Who died and rose again. That is why in antiquity and still today, in many catechumenate centers, the candidates for Baptism are dismissed from the church at the moment when the Eucharistic Action is to begin. [3a]

It is legitimate to regret the preservation of this sign of the Cross and its formula. First because, when it is said after the Entrance Song, the Celebration has already begun.

---

[1] 1 Cor 10, 4; cf. Ex 17, 6; Nm 20, 11.

[2] Mt 21, 42 and parallels; cf. Ps 118, 22; Eph 2, 20.

[3] Jn 1, 51; cf. Gn 28, 10-18.

[3a] This does not seem to be the custom in the United States. [Tr.]

But also because, if we make use of the second (and the most beautiful) of the salutations to the people, of which we shall speak in a moment, we juxtapose two trinitarian invocations, and this is one of those repetitions which the Conciliar *Constitution* had asked to be avoided.

Three Options for Greeting the People

After this the priest greets the people. He may say: "The Lord be with you," which could also be translated by: "The Lord *is* with you." [4] The priest recognizes that he has before him a holy people assembled in the name of Christ, and in whom Christ is present (cf. no. 6: *Presences of Christ*, p. 19).

He is also permitted to use other formulas of greeting that are more solemn, like that with which St. Paul concludes his second letter to the Corinthians: "The grace of our Lord Jesus Christ and the love of God and the fellowship of the Holy Spirit be with you all." The people respond with the words: "And also with you." [4a]

---

[4] After all "Dominus vobiscum" has no verb. And the Dominus tecum" addressed to Mary by the angel at the Annunciation is always translated by "The Lord *is* with you." But by the fact that it is frequently repeated in the course of the Mass, "Dominus vobiscum" appears rather as a wish, hence as if it had a verb in the subjunctive.

[4a] Ever since the Mass has been permitted in the vernacular, there has been a running controversy among scholars concerning the translation of the Latin words *"Et cum spiritu tuo."* The new official English translation is "And also with you." This represents a practical solution, since the English translators did not believe that the meaning attributed to the use of "spirit" (in the translation "And with your spirit") by those who defend it could ever be fully imparted to the people. Hence, they selected a less enigmatic translation.

The author, on the other hand, forms part of the group of scholars who think otherwise and opts for the translation "And with your spirit" (which is incidentally that of France). His reasons are as follows: "This response is not, as is often said, a Semitism signifying simply 'And also with you,' but a recognition of the fact that the priest cannot accomplish the Sacred Action except through the impulse of the Holy Spirit, 'Who unites Himself to his spirit' (cf. Rom 8, 16). It could be translated by 'And may God inspire you.' " A good summary of this whole question will be found in an article by J. B. O'Connell, "Et Cum Spiritu Tuo," in *The Clergy Review*, April 1969, pp. 292-298. [Tr.]

The more developed salutation has the advantage of explicitly evoking the three Persons of the Blessed Trinity not merely in mentioning each one of them, but by describing more precisely their role in our regard. For the Mass is an Action that has a trinitarian structure: it is offered to the glory of the Father, through the priestly mediation of Jesus Christ, in the Holy Spirit, Who is the Principle of unity and holiness because He is the Spirit of love Who unites the Father and the Son, and Who makes Christians participate in that vital union of Father and Son.

We shall find this trinitarian structure of the Mass again in the conclusion of all the Eucharistic Prayers ("Through Him, with Him, in Him. . . ."). In particular, the three new Eucharistic Prayers show, better than the Roman Canon, and as is also done by all the Eastern liturgies, that the "sanctification of the gifts" and our sanctification through them cannot be accomplished without the intervention of the Holy Spirit.

Finally, the priest may also use a third form of greeting: "The grace and peace of God our Father and the Lord Jesus Christ be with you" (Gal 1, 3). The people answer in this case: "Blessed be God, the Father of our Lord Jesus Christ."

13. THE ANTIPHON OF THE ENTRANCE SONG

The Mass forms a unity, as we have said in regard to concelebration (no. 10, p. 29), and we shall have the occasion to repeat it. In a certain way the Mass is always the same because it merely makes present the Unique Sacrifice of Christ. But it makes it present for men who live in diverse periods of time, for changing times and changing men: for a Church which continues to live and develop, which ceaselessly recalls and passes once more through the diverse stages of salvation history.

There is a central uniform core, the recalling of the Last Supper, but it is proper that around it the Mass should present variable parts shedding light in turn on the diverse facets or successive phases of the Mystery of Redemption. This variable part is what has been called "the Proper of the Mass" in contrast with the "Ordinary of the Mass."

The first piece of the Proper of every Mass is the chant that accompanies the entrance of the priest. By its very nature it is indeed a chant, for the Mass is not a mournful memorial; it is a feast, a joyful hence music-accompanied solemnity. Normally, the Entrance Song is a Psalm chosen for its application to the feast or the liturgical season but its most characteristic part is the antiphon. This text may be one that is taken from the Psalm itself or from another book of the Bible, as is the case of the Entrance Song for Christmas Day: "A child is born to us, a son has been given to us . . ." (Is 9, 6).

This *leitmotiv*, with its guiding thought, is repeated periodically between the verses of the Psalm. [5] When the Psalm is completed or rather when the entrance procession is over (since it is a question here of accompaniment whereas the Responsorial Psalm is chanted for itself), the Psalm concludes with the "Glory be to the Father . . ." and the antiphon is sung once more for the last time.

It often happens that the Mass has to be celebrated in a simplified form, or that there is no choir competent to chant the variable parts, [6] even when one sings the parts of the Ordinary. In that case the Entrance Antiphon can no longer play the role of refrain. It is not right to read the Psalm for it is meant to be sung. We shall then content ourselves with reading the antiphon alone for the sake of its content and suggestive power. The priest is also allowed to make a brief comment on it, in order to introduce the assembly directly

---

[5] Concerning the use of the Psalms in Christian prayer, see no. 22, on "the Responsorial Psalm."

[6] It is permissible, however, to sing an Entrance Chant which is common to a series of several Sundays, or also to sing "some canticle or hymn" instead, choosing one that is better known, more popular, and more appropriate.

and vividly into the spirit of the celebration which is beginning.

14. THE PENITENTIAL RITE (CONFESSION OF SINS)

This is an introductory rite which is found in all liturgies in a variety of forms, some of which limp at times. But the recent renewal has desired to structurize as well as simplify it. [7]

The access to a Divine Mystery normally causes in the believer a movement of reserve, a recollection of his wretchedness and hence a desire of purification. The liturgists call the prayers that are born of those sentiments "apologies." The Latin Middle Ages had multiplied "Apology" prayers to excess. Our "Penitential Rite" in the Mass follows a very simple line which in no way hinders its content.

First of all, the presiding priest of the assembly recalls in a sentence that we are all sinners and he invites us to think of our faults in order to be sorry for them and ask pardon.

Everyone examines his conscience during the silence that follows. St. Paul already invited any one who took part in the Lord's Supper "to prove himself before eating this Bread and drinking this Cup" lest he eats and drinks "judgment to himself" (1 Cor 11, 28-29). This is the first of the silences during Mass which are intended to help us make our prayer more personal and profound during the Celebration, and not to return in thought to our worldly business! This silence ought to be sufficiently long to allow us to make a profound examen of conscience. But it should not have the length of an examen in which we must make a detailed survey of our sins.

---

[7] We are thinking of the recent period when the "Prayers at the foot of the altar" seemed to acquire excessive importance and solemnity in the "dialogue Mass," while the sung Mass reduced them to a difficult attempt at dialogue between the priest and the mass servers who were often unable to hear one another properly.

Finally, there is the common confession; all together we confess—which means we proclaim—that we are sinners before God. As sin is not only a personal offense against God but a fault against the community, we proclaim ourselves sinners also before the Church of earth "and to you, my brothers." The priest, who is a sinner as are the faithful, makes his confession together with the whole assembly. The confession thus avoids the more complex dialogue that was formally used, and it presents a more fraternal and communitarian character.

The English translation has tried to avoid useless repetitions and over-emphasis such as "through my most grievous fault." In addition the text has been enriched by mentioning sins "of omission" which formerly did not appear in the Roman Liturgy. We may remark, however, that the Roman Liturgy was more logical, for we sin only by thought, word, and deed and there is no need to add "by omission"; sins of omission fall under one of those three heads, thought, word, and deed. [7a]

It is well for us to say "I confess to God" for it is fundamental now to give our full attention to Him. After honestly acknowledging our wretchedness as sinners, we ask pardon invoking the intercession of the Blessed: "Blessed Mary, ever virgin, all the Angels and Saints," and also the intercession of the Church of earth, which benefits itself from the "communion of saints" though it is composed of sinners: "and you, my brothers."

The "confession" of sins can also make use of other formularies: Biblical verses, or invocations that paraphrase the "Lord, have mercy." In this case there is no need of repeating the latter (as we were accustomed to do at the Kyrie).

[7a] We should note, however, that the English translation side-steps this objection by reworking the original text slightly: "I have sinned through my own fault / in my thoughts and in my words, / in what I have done, / and in what I have failed to do." [Tr.]

Sacramental Which Takes Away Venial Sins

After this common avowal, the priest pronounces the prayer that implores God's pardon: "May almighty God have mercy on us. . . ." It is only a petition for pardon; it is not an absolution properly so-called. The Mass is not meant to replace the Sacrament of Penance which remains necessary for the pardon of grave sins. Nevertheless the Penitential Rite, inserted in the Mass, is a "sacramental" which takes away venial sins, provided we are sorry for them. But this Penitential Rite has no other object than to inspire repentance; it is certainly efficacious for the purification of our conscience.

It would be incorrect to imagine that when the preparatory rite is over, the Mass has no longer anything to do with the pardon of our faults. On the contrary, it is wholly a sacrifice for sins. The consecration of the Precious Blood is done by specifying, as Christ had said, that it is "shed for you and for all men so that sins may be forgiven." The Lamb we immolate will be shown to us as He "Who takes away the sins of the world," and frequently in the course of the Mass, we meet with the expression of our wretchedness, a call for divine mercy, the prayer to be delivered from evil.

15. LORD, HAVE MERCY. GLORY TO GOD

The invocation "Lord have mercy" of our liturgy, is no doubt derived from a litany that is made up of a variety of invocations, and to which the people give a uniform response. It was probably Pope St. Gregory, in the 7th century, who suppressed the litany while preserving the response which from then on remained by itself. Since the Second Vatican Council, the litany has been restored; this is our Universal Prayer. But the threefold "Lord, have mercy" has been preserved at the beginning of Mass. In its simplicity it is a cry that well expresses how wretched we are and that we trust in God.

This is the invocation of those unfortunate people in the Gospel who begged Jesus to cure them or their child. [8] In all these cases the verb has a complement: "have mercy on *me*" or "on *us*." The liturgical formula leaves this out and says: "have mercy." For, after all, it is an imploration for all the miseries of men and not only for our personal miseries. Hence, shortened in its text but unlimited in its object, it is more suitable for a prayer that aims at being catholic, universal.

Lord, Have Mercy: Addressed to Christ

To whom is it addressed? As in the Gospel, it is a supplication that is directed to Christ. But the lepers or the blind, while they called Him "Son of David" or "Lord," saw in Him only the Messiah. For the first Christians, *Kyrios* ("Lord") was a Divine Name, the usual translation of *Yahweh*, and the proper title of the risen and glorious Christ, equal with the Father. [9]

It was in the Middle Ages that a trinitarian extension was given to this invocation, dividing it into three groups of three, and addressing to Christ the three invocations of the second group. The present rules do not oblige us to keep the three-fold repetition. It is certain that an alternating prayer is more easily said if one merely doubles the invocations.

---

[8] There were the blind: Mt 9, 27 and 20, 30-31; Mk 10, 47; the lepers: Lk 17, 13; the Canaanite woman whose daughter was possessed: Mt 15, 22; the father of the epileptic: Mt 17, 14. It is also the prayer that Jesus places on the lips of the publican in the parable: Lk 18, 38.

[9] Let us here mention only two decisive texts. St Peter says, at the end of his discourse on Pentecost (Acts 2, 36): "Let all the House of Israel know most assuredly that God has made both Lord and Christ this Jesus Whom you crucified," and St. Paul, quoting no doubt from a hymn of the early Church (Phil 2, 9-11), says: "God also has exalted Him and has given Him the name that is above every name, so that . . . every tongue should confess that Jesus Christ is Lord."

Gloria: Ancient Jewel of Christian Prayer

"Glory to God in the highest" is one of the most ancient jewels of our prayer. It is possible that it is our *Gloria* which Pliny the Younger speaks about in his letter to the emperor Trajan in 112, when he says that the Christians "sing to Christ as to a God." Together with the *Te Deum*, it is one of the very rare specimens left us of the non-biblical psalms inspired by the Bible which were sung by the first Christians. [10]

The *Gloria* is Biblically inspired for it begins with the song of the Angels at Christmas. It continues with short acclamations of praise addressed first to the Father, then to the Son, and ends with a trinitarian formula.

Originally, this chant no doubt belonged to the Office of Matins (as today the *Te Deum* is sung at the end of Matins). The *Gloria* was introduced in the Mass on major Feasts, and also when the celebrant was the bishop. It gradually became used almost daily, which has resulted in making it commonplace and robbing it of its festive character; if there is a feast every day there are no longer any feasts! That is why we can be grateful that it is used more rarely according to the new regulations of the Mass of *Today*.

---

[10] *"Psalmoi idiotikoi,"* i.e., particular, not official Psalms. St Paul is possibly alluding to them when he invites Christians to admonish one another by psalms inspired by the Spirit as well as by "hymns and spiritual songs" (Col 3, 16).

SOME REMARKS WITH RESPECT TO TRANSLATIONS

Lord, have mercy. Some accustomed to hear "Lord, have mercy on us" in litanies, may have been annoyed at this omission of the "us." It is well to note, first of all that *Lord, have mercy* exactly translates the two-word *Kyrie eleison* which leaves out any complement of the verb. When the text has a complement, for instance, in the *Gloria* and the *Lamb of God (Agnus Dei)*, it is then translated by "have mercy *on us.*"

"Peace. . . . His people on earth" is also a translation that is perfectly exact, whereas the usual translation "to men of goodwill" is not right. The "goodwill" of which the original Greek text speaks, and even the Latin text, is the *goodwill, the kindness, the love of God toward men.*

We know that Protestant versions mostly read "goodwill to men" and this means simply that God loves men. We westerners should not follow our reasoning propensities that might lead us to say God does not love all.

Similarly, in the formula of Consecration where the Blood is said to be "shed for many" it is necessary to note that no one is excluded by that indefinite expression; hence, the English has: "shed . . . for all men."

Another version of the "Glory to God" *(Gloria)*, and one that is somewhat crystallized to make it more singable, could avoid difficulties caused by the present text. We could adopt a translation which is less certain from the standpoint of the Gospel text but is traditional with the Orientals and was moreover adopted by Luther (cf. J. A. Jungmann, *Missarum Solemnia*). It reads: "Glory to God in the highest, peace on earth, goodwill to men."

16. "LET US PRAY TOGETHER" (COLLECT)

The Introductory Rites end with prayer, with the first Oration which is often called the "Collect."

Prayer in its widest sense is a raising of mind and heart to God Who we know loves us. It is a movement of the soul tending to commune spiritually with God, by raising to Him sentiments (such as love, gratitude), and mediations (intercessions).

It would be strange indeed if up to this point in the Mass we had not prayed in that sense! In fact we have been doing nothing else; the Entrance Song offered a theme or motive of prayer which could then develop and grow stronger in the Psalm; in the Penitential Rite, we prayed God to grant us pardon for our faults; then "Lord have mercy" and "Glory to God in the highest" were alternatively a supplication with a recognition of God's glory and thanksgiving. The rest of the Mass contains numerous prayers.

We even can say that the whole Mass is a Prayer, the Great Prayer of the Church. No doubt we define the Mass as an offering and a sacrifice, but are those supreme acts of religious homage not, as it were, the incarnation of prayer, its manifestation by indubitable signs? Finally, even when we merely welcome God's gifts during Mass, when we listen to His Word or receive His Supersubstantial Bread, is it not necessary for us to do it in an interior attitude of humility and readiness which is a fundamental attitude of prayer?

> The faithful in virtue of their royal priesthood join in the offering of the Eucharist. They likewise exercise that priesthood in receiving the Sacraments, *in prayer* and thanksgiving, in the witness of a holy life. . . .
>
> Therefore all the disciples of Christ, persevering in prayer and praising God, should present themselves as a living sacrifice, holy and pleasing to God" *(Constitution on the Church,* art. 10).

Priests . . . must instruct the faithful to participate in
the celebrations of the Sacred Liturgy in such a way that
they become proficient in genuine prayer *(Decree on the
Ministry and Life of Priests*, art. 5).

Official Prayer of People of God

But all this does not mean that in the Mass there are no
moments when prayer manifests itself in a more special and
official way. This is the case of Orations. This word comes
from the Latin *oratio,* which means first a discourse, a
speech. We used to speak about funeral orations in this
sense. In our liturgical Orations a prayer is expressed solemnly by the priest in the name of all. But how can the priest
be truly the interpreter of a great number of diverse needs
of each individual who assists at Mass?

It is impossible to answer this question except by stressing
the importance of what precedes the Oration properly so-
called: the invitation to prayer, followed by a silence.

"Let us pray" is a short expression and it might pass almost unperceived. The imperative in the first person plural
is often used to indicate banal actions: Let's go!" or "Let us
see!" How much weightier is "Let us pray!" This is so first
of all because praying is an activity which is difficult, which
demands a certain effort. Secondly, in this call the plural is
not one of majesty nor a plural of familiarity, as is often the
case in the expression "Let us see!" or "Let's go!"

It is a plural which implies the whole mystery of the People of God, of that People's priesthood and the priesthood of
its ministers. The priest invites the other faithful—for the
priest, being himself baptized, forms part of the faithful—
to exercise their baptismal priesthood by prayer. His role as
minister at the service of the community not only allows him
to express this invitation, but it also gives him the right to
gather together all the individual prayers and present them
to the Father, as we offer several flowers in a bouquet. The
term "Collect" which still designates the first Oration, no

doubt evokes, in an indirect way, this function of the priest to "collect" the individual petitions in one single "Oration" which becomes the Oration of the Church. [11]

People Need Time to Formulate Petitions

But it is indispensable, if we want the gathering together of prayers to have a real content, that we let each individual have the time to formulate his petitions. This is the purpose of the silence, which is relatively prolonged, now following the invitation "Let us pray." This "Let us pray" loses all its meaning if the time of silence is too reduced or is practically suppressed. For what can be the reason for the priest to say "Let *us* pray" if he immediately starts praying alone in a loud voice?

Besides, if we look closely at the content of the Collect, that is, the text which the Missal makes the priest recite, we realize that it often confines itself to saying to God: "Hear, (or: grant) the prayers of Your family," and this makes sense only if said family has actually prayed.

It is here first of all that the faithful exercise "active participation." Let them bring to the Mass their pains, their cares, the concerns of their family, their lawful, professional, apostolic ambitions. Without that, the priest offers to God only a majestic but empty formula.

17. STRUCTURE AND CONTENT OF THE ORATION

All the Orations of the Roman Mass have the same structure. It is easy to discern three parts in them: the address, the petition, and the conclusion.

---

[11] In fact, the historians of the Mass have different opinions regarding the precise origin of the term *Collecta* or *Collectio* that is frequently given to the First Oration. It is possible that that name was derived from the fact that it was pronounced *super (plebem) collectam* (over the people assembled). In this sense it is truly the conclusion of the *Introductory Rites* (cf. Jungmann, *op. cit,* II, 119; also N.M. Denis-Boulet, in Martimort, *L'Eglise en prière,* 3rd ed., p. 347).

The Address

The *address* designates the Father with a few very sober words: "God" or "Lord almighty" or "Most powerful and merciful Lord." Spontaneously a Christian would address his prayer rather to Christ. The Liturgy honors this desire. As we have seen, 'Lord, have mercy" is addressed to Christ. Several invocations of the *Gloria* directly refer to Christ. So also the acclamation of the people after the Consecration. Then, at the moment of Communion, the "Lamb of God" and the preparatory prayers.

Nevertheless, the Mass, in its fundamental structure, is addressed to the Father, through the mediation of the Son, in the unity of the Holy Spirit. Some modern Orations, or Orations that have been modified, are addressed to the Son. Habitually, they have been corrected in order to be brought in line with the general rule: to the Father through the Son.

This address is sometimes more developed. On the occasion of a major feast, or even for the anniversary of a Saint, the petition rests on a motive that is connected with the address by a relative sentence: "God Who, this day, by the light of the Holy Spirit have instructed Your Church . . ."; "God, Who have offered to the human race the treasures of eternal life through the virginal Maternity of the Virgin Mary." The official translation of those two last Orations (Pentecost, January 1st) has done away with the ponderousness of relative propositions (of which we have given an example) by reestablishing these prayers in their earlier form.

The Petition

Even in such cases of special major feasts and anniversaries of Saints, the *petition* remains very general. This is as it should be since, as we have already said, each individual has been given the opportunity to formulate his particular petitions during the silence that has followed the invitation to pray. We might wish for Orations that are more specific, more actual, more living. But it is evident that in such a case they could no longer serve for a prayer *in common*.

If the Liturgy wishes to express itself in the name of all, if it wants to avoid restricting itself to particular petitions, as well as to refrain from using expressions that seem too fervent to be in harmony with the religious level or dispositions of a whole assembly, it must confine itself to formulas that seem relatively cold and abstract; and, of course, sobriety is a characteristic of the Roman genius as is so very evident in the Roman Liturgy.

Many Orations have undergone changes or have been replaced by others during the recent reform of the Missal. Formulas which deserve to be called "hackneyed" have been done away with, or again petitions which today have become unreal have been eliminated. For example, too many Orations, during Lent, insisted on a regime of fasting which is no longer practiced except spontaneously. Others asked for the grace to "despise earthly realities," which could be interpreted as expressing a spirituality that tries to evade our secular duties.

In spite of their seeming coldness, these Orations nevertheless contain real treasures of genuine piety, which we must know how to discover under the modest clothing of their conciseness. A simple hearing of them in the course of the Celebration will not enable us to discover and appreciate this value. (We see here once more a good reason for owning and using a hand Missal in which these precious prayers are presented to us for our devout consideration—Tr.). We must take the time to "ponder them in our heart" and learn to relish them.

The Conclusion

The *conclusion presents* the petitions to the Father through the priestly mediation of His Son. The Church has for a long time striven to avoid even the appearance of favoring

Arianism in treating Jesus as if He were a simple mediator, inferior to the Father. [12] To counteract this error, the
Church has accumulated professions of faith in the Divinity
of Christ. "Through Jesus Christ, *Your Son, our Lord, Who
lives and reigns, God, with You* in the unity of the Holy Spirit,
forever and ever."

We might note that the *Deus* of the Latin formula, or *God*
in the English, is really superfluous, for all the expressions
which go before express the equivalent of this truth.

It was difficult to lessen this ponderousness without seeming to take something away from our profession of faith in
the Divinity of Jesus. Hence, this developed (long) formula
has been retained for the Collect which is the principal Oration of the Mass. But for the other two Orations, the one over
the gifts and the other that follows Communion, it was considered sufficient to use the short conclusion "through Christ
our Lord."

Amen: The People's Assent

Whether long or short, the conclusion of the Oration calls
for the acclamation of the People who will say: *Amen.* Hence,
the formula said by the priest alone, but preceded by the
silent prayer of the people and followed by the acclamation
which expresses their assent, really belongs to the assembled
people.

The people will also say *Amen* frequently during the course
of the Mass. We shall postpone the explanation of this word
Amen, a term so rich in meaning, to the *Amen* whose meaning is least understood, the one said by the faithful when the

---

[12] Arianism, we may recall, was a heresy during the first centuries
of Christianity which professed that Christ was an ordinary creature,
a man who became son of God by adoption, instead of holding the
true doctrine which affirms that He is Son of God by nature, from all
eternity.

"Body of Christ" is presented to them (no. 42). Let us simply note here that the term does not have the meaning of resignation which makes us say, "O.K." or "all right"; it means instead an enthusiastic acclamation. No doubt it is an assent to a petition or demand, but it also ratifies the glorification of Christ which has been formulated in the conclusion.

THE LITURGY OF THE WORD

III

18. THE WORD AND THE MYSTERY OF FAITH

The Collect was at the same time summit and conclusion of the Introductory Rites. Immediately after this begins the Liturgy of the Word. It would be very wrong to believe that this too is a preliminary, as if the Eucharistic Liturgy were the only one that has importance. This led to the fact that the first part of the Liturgy was for a long time known as the "Fore-Mass," [1] which seemed to make the Liturgy of the Word a mere external prelude to the Mass properly so-called.

This unacceptable division was confirmed by a casuistry which is still accepted in our own day by too many Catholics: It suffices to arrive before the Offertory in order to be able to say: "Yes, I assisted at Mass and have satisfied my Sunday obligation!"

Of course, we can thus give comfort to a person who by accident has come late. But if we, on principle, regard the Liturgy of the Word as a simple Introduction from which we are perfectly free to dispense ourselves, this is an inadmissible abuse which reveals a total misunderstanding of the very nature of Christianity and its Sacraments.

---

[1] Jungmann justly criticizes the use of another faulty expression "the Mass of the Catechumens" to designate this first part of the Mass, and yet he talks afterwards about the "Mass of the faithful." In both these expressions the word "Mass," in Latin *missa*, keeps its etymological meaning of "dis*missal*." But by admitting that the word "Mass" can designate that which precedes the dismissal, we realize that the two expressions are unfortunate. First of all because the faithful also assisted at the first part of the Mass. And then, as Jungmann remarks, because the catechumens were dismissed before the Universal Prayer (the Prayer of the Faithful) which, as we shall see, was reserved for the baptized. The Universal Prayer is the conclusion and the summit of the Liturgy of the Word!

Intimate Bond between Word and Eucharist

It is not for reasons of ecclesiastical discipline and the morality governing matters of worship that we insist on this point. It is because the Gospel itself teaches us how intimate is the bond which unites the Mystery of the Word and the Mystery of the Eucharist. In particular, the miracle of the multiplication of the loaves shows this unity. We know that this miracle is a prefiguration of the Eucharist. Not only is it a question in both cases of loaves with which Jesus gives superabundant food to large crowds, but there are also numerous details, in the account of the miracle, which show that the evangelists were thinking of the celebration of the Last Supper. [2]

Here is the way St. Mark (6, 34) introduces the account of this miracle: "When he landed, Jesus saw a large crowd, and had compassion on them, because they were like sheep without a shepherd." This means not only that they have no guide but that they have no food, for the function of a shepherd is not to lead the sheep aimlessly but to lead them to verdant and abundant pastures. [3] But does this mean that Christ's compassion for the multitude will make Him hurry to give them bread? We read that "He began to teach them many things."

Jesus is the Savior of the world, the Savior of men. Of course, He saves us by His Cross and His Resurrection, the Paschal Mystery of His passover from death to life, which He communicates to us through His Sacraments. But He

---

[2] Jesus "takes" the loaves, "gives thanks" (*eucharistesas*), "pronounces the blessing," "breaks the loaves." All these terms are found again in the account of the Last Supper and in the actual words of the Consecration. In the Roman Canon it is added that he does this while "looking up to heaven," a detail that is found in the account of the multiplication of the loaves (Mt 14, 19; Mk 6, 41; Lk 9, 16), but not in the account of the Last Supper. But this "looking up" of Jesus is also noted by St. John at the resurrection of Lazarus (11, 5), and at the beginning of the great "priestly prayer" (17, 1) which has a clear Eucharistic tonality.

[3] Cf. Ps 23, 1-3, 5; Ez 34, 14; etc.

saves us first by His Word, if we cling to it by faith. Jesus often concludes His discourses with this apostrophe: "He who has ears to hear, let him hear!" [4]

Miraculous cures are "signs" like the Sacraments and they are the physical signs of the spiritual effects produced by the Sacraments. To accomplish such miracles, Christ demands faith before anything else, or He even declares that it is faith which works the desired cure. [5] In Nazareth, if He "cannot" work miracles, it is because His fellow citizens are wanting in faith, and He Himself "wondered at their lack of faith" (cf. Mk 6, 5).

Faith is the source-principle, the root of salvation. The Sacraments are Sacraments of faith," [6] that is, "signs of faith." They demand faith in order to be operative and, in addition, "they foster faith." [7]

The celebration of a Sacrament thus entails as an essential element the recalling of this Word of God which is at the same time the principal motive and the object of our faith. [8]

Difference between "Believing" and "Practicing" Christians

Today a distinction is often made—one that would have appeared monstrous to the Apostles and the First Christians —between "believing" and "practicing" Christians or Catholics. There are many "believers" but a very small number of "practicing" Christians.

Yet it is difficult to know what is meant by "believers." Among them there are no doubt some who accept the beliefs of Christianity without going deeply into them; their so-called

[4] Mt 11, 15; 13, 9. 43; Mk 4, 23; 7, 16; 8, 18; Lk 14, 35, and parallels.
[5] Cf. Mt 8, 10. 26; 9, 2. 22. 28-29; 15, 28; etc.
[6] This is what St. Thomas usually called them.
[7] *Constitution on the Sacred Liturgy*, art. 59.
[8] That is why the renewed rite of Baptism, even for small children, comprises a celebration of the Word, which, evidently, is intended for the parents and those who assist at the Sacrament, not the baby presented for Baptism.

faith may be merely an opinion and even a rather negative
one. They do not reject the faith of their Baptism, and sometimes they pray for help to a God Who is rather vague.

But among these "non-practicing believers" there are no
doubt also true believers, that is, baptized persons who cling
profoundly to the principal dogmas, pray often and possibly
read Holy Scripture, but who by a strangely twisted reasoning, do not take part in worship and do not go to the Sacraments because they look upon these things as a simple for-
mality, and fail to recognize their vivifying role. Or again
they may dislike the liturgical gatherings because they reject
a "visible" Church which has institutions that can be seen
and heard, or simply because they are thoughtless, distracted,
negligent people.

For some time now another category of Christians has
made its appearance; it is comprised of "practicing non-
believers." These are certainly not hypocrites. They think
they are believers. But their faith is asleep, it suffers from
spiritual sclerosis.

This sleepiness and this hardening of spiritual arteries are
fostered by their way of practicing their religion. They go to
the Sacraments as one goes to an insurance agency, so as
to feel sure their conscience is in order; they look upon them
as efficacious, though incomprehensible, means guaranteeing
eternal salvation.

Since they think they have found God, they have for a
long time stopped seeking Him. They receive the Sacraments without reflecting that these are not only remedies
and instruments of salvation, but *Mysteries* which we must
contemplate. They fail to realize that the Sacraments are
not intended to recompense an inert and scarcely meritorious faith but to arouse, spur on, and foster ever more and
more a faith which is constantly more living and more demanding.

Such persons, evidently, imagine that the Liturgy of the
Word is quite useless as a preparation for this Eucharist in

which they see only a sort of spiritual super-vitamin pill containing Divine energy. Otherwise, how is it possible to approach the Eucharist which is the "mystery of faith," as is proclaimed at every Consecration ("Let us proclaim the mystery of faith"), without opening ourselves and our faith more and more by listening to and assimilating the Word of God?

The Mass Is a Unity

The Liturgy of the Word is a necessary preparation for the Liturgy of the Eucharist if we want to prevent our faith, which is the first and essential condition for salvation, from becoming anemic and degenerating into some conventional "religious practice." Such a practice would reduce Christianity to an ensemble of recipes as are found also in fetishistic religions, whereas it is a discovery of the infinite God and of His plan of love for us, a "worship in spirit and in truth" (Jn 4, 24).

19. THE BREAD OF LIFE

It is not sufficient for us to see in the Liturgy of the Word a necessary preparation for the Liturgy of the Eucharist, but one with a totally different nature, as if we had first to attend a seance of indoctrination before being able to profit better from the Eucharist, or as if we had the obligation of following a lesson in the catechism before the Mass properly so-called.

This, first of all, is contrary to the facts which are shown us by the Liturgy of the past and the Liturgy of *today*. Our Liturgy of the Word is derived from the offices in the Jewish Synagogue, which were self-sufficient and did not terminate in a sacrifice. [9]

---

[9] We might mention here that the sacrifices were celebrated only in the Temple. The synagogues were, as the term *syn-agoge* indicates, places of gatherings, which appeared after the first destruction of the Temple, in the dispersion (among the Jews outside Palestine). Still to this day, since the Temple is destroyed, Judaism no longer has sacrifices and its worship is reduced to a celebration of the Word (comprising readings, homily, and prayers).

Most of the rites of Christian antiquity have known celebrations of the Word that were held for their own sake and did not issue into the Eucharist, as well as Eucharistic celebrations which were not immediately preceded by a Liturgy of the Word. This is still so today. The conciliar *Constitution* recommends "sacred celebrations of the Word of God" that are held for themselves, and in no way used as preliminaries for a Eucharist. [10]

On the other hand, today there are no Masses which begin directly with the preparation of the Eucharistic gifts. What might happen is that the Liturgy of the Word, instead of being taken from the Missal of the day, is taken from a Sacrament like Baptism, Confirmation, or Orders, whose celebration, which comprises readings, then constitutes the first part of the Mass.

The Mystery of the Two Tables

This should help us understand that the Liturgy of the Word is more than just the preparation for the Eucharist which we emphasized in the preceding chapter. There exists between these two celebrations a relationship of profound analogy which can be expressed by a saying that has become classical: the mystery of the Two tables.

The Imitation of Christ, [11] states the following:

> There are two things without which I cannot live a good life: the Word of God, light of my soul, and His Sacrament, the Bread of life. We are even permitted to say that they are two tables placed one here and one there in the treasure-room of Holy Church.

---

[10] Cf. Art. 35, par. 4. In the Instruction *Inter Oecumenici*: three articles are consecrated to such celebrations, sometimes called Bible services. Some take the place of Mass where its celebration is not possible because there are no priests available (art. 37). Others (art. 38) are gatherings for readings and prayers. In both cases, their plan must be similar to that of the Liturgy of the Word in the Mass.

[11] Book 4, ch. 11.

One table is that of the altar on which there is found the consecrated Bread, the precious Body of Christ.

The other is that of the Divine Law, which contains the Sacred Doctrine, forming us in true faith and leading us surely and safely even inside the veil, where there is found the Holy of holies. . . .

Bossuet has magnificently orchestrated this theme: [12]

There, the ministers of sacred things speak to God in the name of the people; here, they speak to the people in the name of God; there, Jesus Christ is adored in the truth of His Body; here, He causes Himself to be recognized in the truth of His doctrine. . . . There, through the efficaciousness of the Holy Spirit and by mystical words . . . [13] the gifts that have been presented are transformed into the Body of our Lord Jesus Christ; here, through the same Spirit, still by the power of the Divine Word, the faithful of Jesus Christ must be secretly transformed so as to be made His Body and His members.

This theme of the Two Tables, not only successive and complementary, but analogous and comparable, belongs to the most constant tradition of the Fathers, which the *Constitution On Divine Revelation* of Vatican Council II thus summarizes: [14]

The Church has always venerated the Divine Scriptures just as she venerates the Body of the Lord, since, especially in the sacred Liturgy, *she unceasingly receives and offers to the faithful the Bread of Life from the table both of God's Word and of Christ's Body.*

Discourse on the Bread of Life

The expression "Bread of Life," which applies to the two elements, shows that this theme of the two tables has its origin in the Gospel of St. John, chapter 6, where is found

---

[12] Lenten Discourse of 1661, Exordium.

[13] Mystical means here that which is connected with the Mystery, with the Sacrament.

[14] Article 21 (*italics added*).

the discourse customarily called "the discourse on the bread of life." We must pause on this point for a little while in order to draw forth a doctrine which is truly essential for anyone who wishes to delve deeply into the Eucharistic Mystery.

This chapter of St. John's Gospel begins with an account of the multiplication of the loaves. [15] As in the other evangelists, we notice "Eucharistic" details: Jesus distributes the loaves, then the fishes, "after having given thanks" (eucharistesas.) But only from John do we learn that this miracle took place a short time before the Feast of the Pasch, which suggests a relationship with the Last Supper and Christ's passage (passover) to His Father (Jn 13, 1). John alone notes that this miracle aroused the enthusiasm of the crowd which recognized in Jesus "the prophet who is to come into the world" (Jn 6, 14). This means the prophet announced by Moses and similar to the latter (cf. Dt 18, 15. 18).

Quite naturally, the Jews must have compared Jesus with Moses, who had fed the people in the desert by the miracle of the manna. Jesus then withdraws into the mountain to prevent them from proclaiming Him king—this too is a detail that is proper to John's account. Christ refuses this attachment to His person which is inspired by purely material interests.

Hence, when the crowd finds Him again in Capernaum, the following day, He tries to make them ascend to a higher plane: "You seek Me . . . because you have eaten of the loaves and have been filled. Labor, not to get the food that perishes but for that which endures unto life everlasting, which the Son of Man will give you" (Jn 6, 26-27).

Let us note immediately that in John, and particularly in this discourse, "life everlasting" or "the life" is not life in the hereafter, but Divine life which man already shares in

---

[15] It is generally thought that there are two miracles of the multiplication of the loaves. The first recalled by the four evangelists, the second by Matthew and Mark alone. But these six accounts coincide in numerous points.

here below. We shall see that it is, already on earth, the fruit of faith.

"What are we to do that we may perform the works of God?" asks the crowd which, as so often in St. John, is shown to be moving on the wrong track after hearing an ambiguous word of the Master. And to this He gives this astonishing reply: "This is the work of God, that you believe in Him Whom He has sent" (Jn 6, 28-29). To believe is "the work of God," both because faith is a gift of God and because faith unites man to God. This expression gives the *leitmotiv*, the guiding theme, of the whole lengthy discourse that will follow.

Theme of Word and Eucharist

It has been asked if this discourse has only the Word as its theme, or if the one theme is the Eucharist. Certain interpreters have thought that it is first concerned with the Word, and that it is directed to the Eucharist beginning with verse 51. In reality, it is wholly concerned with the faith in the Word, which finds its accomplishment in the Eucharist, the Mystery of faith.

A Biblical theme will constitute the bond between the Word and the Eucharist: that of the manna. This was "bread from heaven," somewhat like "bread [come from the abode] of the angels." [16] This means food (for "bread," in the Bible, often has this general meaning) which is granted miraculously by God to sustain His people as they march through the desert. Because it comes from heaven, it is often compared to rain, snow, hail. [17] These comparisons are used also for the Word of God. [18]

Already Deuteronomy showed the superiority of the Word over the manna: "Not by bread alone does man live, but by every word that comes forth from the mouth of the Lord" (Dt 8, 3). And Jesus will make use of this text in the desert

---

[16] Ex 16, 4, 14ff; Wis 16, 20, Ps 78, 24ff; quoted by Jn 6, 31.

[17] Ps 78, 23-24, but especially Ps 147, 16-18.

[18] Ps 147, 15, but especially Is 55, 10-11.

in rejecting the temptation to perform a miracle for a purely material motive and against the will of God (Mt 4, 4).

Manna was miraculous because of its origin, but its power was natural: it merely nourished bodies, it did not give *"the life"* (Jn 6, 49. 58). On the contrary, the "bread of life" that has come down from heaven is Jesus Christ Himself, Who personally is the Word of the Father, the Word (Jn 1, 1-18) Whom we assimilate by faith, so much so that this Bread, this Jesus Christ, already gives us Divine life here below: "Moses did not give you the bread from heaven, but My Father gives you the true bread from heaven. For the bread of God is that which comes down from heaven (cf. Jn 3, 13) and gives life to the world" (vv. 32-33).

After this Jesus states clearly: "I am the Bread of Life" (v. 35) and He will repeat it: "I am the Bread of Life" (v. 48). "I am the living Bread that has come down from heaven" (v. 51). Let us remember that in St. John, Jesus frequently says "I am" to insinuate His Divine nature, for "I am" is the Name of God revealed to Moses in the burning bush on Mount Horeb. [20]

The Bread of Life Is Jesus

The Bread of Life, the Bread that has come down from heaven, is therefore the Person of Jesus, but also at the same time His Word, His message. Very soon after this, Jesus would say something that was still more extraordinary: it is necessary to eat His Flesh and drink His Blood, that is, one must adhere to His humanity, for "flesh-and-blood" among the Jews designated the limited and fragile human condition (Mt 16, 17). But this adhesion or steady attachment will not be achieved only through faith, for His Body is

[19] Cf Jn 1, 4; 3, 15-16; 10, 10, etc.

[20] Ex 3, 14. In St. John: "I am the light of the world" (8, 12; 9, 5); "the door of the sheep" (10, 8); "the good shepherd" (10, 11); "the resurrection" (11, 25); "the Way, the Truth, and the Life" (14, 6); "the true Vine" (15, 1). But also "I am" by itself (8, 24. 28. 58).

truly food and His Blood is truly drink. And the banquet prepared by Jesus [21] has a sacrificial value: "The bread that I
will give is My Flesh for the life of the world" (v. 51).

The Jews (v. 52) and then the disciples themselves found
such language intolerable (v. 60), no doubt because they interpreted it in an overly materialistic sense. They refused to
believe, and this refusal was the occasion for the announcement of the treason of Judas (vv. 64. 71). To this Jesus reacts
in a surprising fashion. He Who invited men to eat His Flesh
(v. 63), now says: "It is the spirit that gives life; the Flesh
profits nothing [that is, by itself alone, separately from the
spirit, and from faith in the Word]. The words that I have
spoken to you are spirit and life."

But it is throughout this discourse that Jesus returns to
the themes of faith (vv. 29. 35. 40. 47) and inner instruction
(v. 45). And the conclusion is the confession of faith of Peter
in the name of the disciples who had remained faithful:
"Lord, to whom shall we go? You have words of everlasting
life, and we have come to believe and to know that You are
the Christ, the Son of God" (vv. 68-69).

Nevertheless, the Bread of Life is designated as real food
and this is not said in a metaphorical way, for it is the seed
of the bodily resurrection (v. 54), while at the same time it
realizes a profound and vital union with Jesus, Who is Himself vitally united with the Father (vv. 56-57).

Hence, an attentive reading of this discourse, which is
surprisingly unified but also complex, will convince us that
the Word and the Eucharist are neither opposed to one other
nor part of different domains. They are in reality complementary, organically united, and lead to Life, through and
with one other. The Liturgy of the Word leads to the Eu-

---

[21] Evoking implicitly "the banquet of Wisdom," cf. Prv 9, 1-6 (Jesus
designates Himself as Wisdom in Matthew 11, 19), which should be
compared with Is 55, 1-3 and the parables of the banquets (Mt 22, 1-14;
Lk 14, 1-24).

charist, not in virtue of a simple succession but by an inner dynamism. Moreover, as we shall see, it is by the word of Jesus that the Eucharist is consecrated.

20. "TO OPEN TREASURES OF THE BIBLE"

If the Second Vatican Council was characterized by a wonderful ecumenical spirit, this resulted in the first place from the fact that beginning with the first sessions consecrated to the Liturgy it affirmed the primacy of the Word of God in the life of the Church, in her faith, and in her prayer. Nothing could have been more pleasing to our "separated brethren" than such an attitude.

The *Constitution on the Sacred Liturgy* (art. 24) declared that not only does the Liturgy use Scripture by drawing its Readings from it, but it is also inspired by Scripture in its language; and even more important though less evident, the Liturgy takes "its elan," its inspiration, from Scripture and its "actions and signs derive their meaning" from it. Thus to achieve the restoration, progress, and adaptation of the sacred Liturgy, it is essential to promote that warm and living love for Scripture to which the venerable tradition of both Eastern and Western rites [and Christian families] gives testimony.

One of the practical means, cited by the *Constitution,* to promote this "warm and living love for Scripture," is that "the treasures of the Bible are to be opened up more lavishly, so that richer fare may be provided for the faithful at *the table of God's Word*" (art. 51) and in particular, "in sacred celebrations there is to be more reading from the Scripture, and it is to be more varied and suitable" (art. 35, par. 1).

Hence, at Mass, in order to "open the treasures of the Bible" more fully "a more representative portion of the Holy Scriptures will be read to the people in the course of a prescribed number of years" (art. 51).

The New Lectionary

It is in obedience to this last rule that the new Lectionary [22] has been promulgated and is now in effect. The most striking feature about it is the riches of this "table of the Word."

An exhaustive analysis is out of the question in a book of this sort. We will content ourselves to indicate merely its most salient characteristics.

Each day of the liturgical year has its own Readings, which are arranged in two different ways:

The 34 Sundays after the Epiphany and after Pentecost which form only one series, as well as the weekdays of this period, have a "continuous" or "semi-continuous" reading; the texts are not chosen so much for their content as for giving the faithful a more complete and balanced idea of the principal books of the Bible.

During the major seasons of the liturgical year (Advent-Christmas-Epiphany, Lent, Easter Time), the texts are chosen so as to shed light on the Mystery that is being celebrated. The same applies to major feasts.

The *Sundays* of all the liturgical seasons have their Readings distributed over a cycle of three years. This was necessary first of all in order that "a more representative portion of the Holy Scriptures will be read to the people in the course of a prescribed number of years" (art. 51). Thanks to the extended character of this cycle, the majority of the faithful, who go to Mass only on Sundays, will hear almost the entire Gospels.

Moreover, this seems more in keeping with a phenomenon of our epoch, namely, the acceleration of time. For a Chris-

---

[22] A book which contains the Readings to be made in the Liturgy. Here we are speaking only of the Lectionary for Mass. There is also a Lectionary for the Divine Office (popularly called the Breviary) which is independent of the one for Mass, although the Lectionaries for the various Sacraments can be used during the Mass in which these Sacraments (for example, Matrimony or Confirmation) or sacramentals (for example, funerals or religious professions) are celebrated.

tian of the 17th or the 18th century, the annual returns of
the parables of the Good Samaritan or of the Unjust Steward
seemed to have a much greater distance between them than
to a Christian of our jet age! [23]

Finally, the riches of the Biblical treasures are further ex-
ploited by the fact—one that brings us back to the ancient
Roman tradition—that there are three Readings for Sundays
and major feasts: first, a Reading from the Old Testament
(except during the Easter season when the first reading is
taken from the Acts of the Apostles: the Passover of Christ
and Pentecost which is its development have inaugurated a
new era); and then a Reading from the Epistles or letters of
the Apostles; and, finally, the Gospel Reading.

Some may object that three Readings are a heavy burden
and lengthen the Mass. This is an *a priori* view and will most
likely not be confirmed by experience. Those who have a
serious reason for fearing such inconveniences are permitted, with the prior permission of the Bishops' Conference,
to use only two Readings, the second being always the Gospel.

Positive Reaction to New Readings

However, experience has already shown that the inconvenience involved in the extra Reading is even less than might
be expected. Here is the testimony of two priests who were
permitted to use three Readings in their parishes by way of
experiment:

Is it true that three Readings make the Mass too long?
It lasts three or four minutes longer and it is scarcely
noticeable. . . . The texts of the new Lectionary are not
long and the Eucharistic Prayer is shorter. In any case,
the faithful are not complaining about the length of our
Masses.

---

[23] This is true for adults, not children. For psychological as well as
physiological reasons a day or a year seems very long to children. So
it might be well to consider the advantages of a special Lectionary for
children.

The texts of the Epistles and sometimes those of the Gospel are difficult for people to understand. Does not adding another Reading seem to magnify this difficulty?

It is true that even in the new Lectionary the texts are not always easy to understand. But we must take the Word of God as it exists. It obliges us, priests, to renew our knowledge of the Bible. We will encounter Old Testament texts that are not so well known. It will prove enriching for us to get to work and understand them properly.

In the beginning especially, the faithful found the texts difficult, but they are getting accustomed to them now. Some are very well disposed toward the new Lectionary because they come in contact with some very beautiful texts, especially in the Old Testament. It is always necessary to give some explanations. The priest who gives the Homily prepares, and sometimes himself makes, the preliminary explanations for each one of the texts. [24]

21. "HE SPOKE THROUGH THE PROPHETS"

Most Catholics have little or no knowledge of the Old Testament. The Lectionary will enable them to discover it. But, perhaps, they think they can do very well without it. What good is this ancient history, which has so completely been devaluated by the New Testament, and notably by the Gospel?

We must reject such arguments for they are totally valueless. Our Lord Himself has said formally, regarding the Old Law, that He had "not come to abolish [it] but to fulfill [it]," that is, to bring it to perfection (Mt 5, 17). How can we understand the New Law if we do not know what is presupposed by its fulfillment or bringing to perfection? It would be like studying a cut flower and refusing to take notice of its stem and its roots.

When we read the Gospel in a fine edition, we are struck by the numerous texts in bold characters or italics, the foot-

---

[24] *Semaine Religieuse* d'Angers [*Religious Week* of Angers], February 1969, pp. 104-108.

notes or marginal notes which constantly refer to the Old
Testament; images, words, whole sentences are literally borrowed from those Books that have come to us from the time
before Christ.

We must say that a person has a very insufficient, very
poor, and very superficial knowledge of the Gospel if he does
not know the overtones which, already in the Law and the
Prophets, sounded in words like: banquet, supper, manna,
lamb, shepherd, vine, Pasch, temptation (or trial), water,
thirst, heart. . . .

To take a couple of examples among many others, we
should have but a superficial understanding of the account
of the Annunciation if we did not recognize in it, as in a fili-
gree, the prophecy of Nathan to David (2 Sm 7), and the
promise of a son made to Abraham and to Sarah (Gn 18, 14).
A person who is unacquainted with the Canticle of Anna, the
mother of Samuel (1 Sm 2, 1-10), and Psalm 112 misses much
of the appreciation of the *Magnificat* which is a rich echo of
these ancient songs; the same is true of the person for whom
"the promises made to Abraham and to his seed forever"
are perfectly meaningless.

It might be objected that long studies would be necessary
if we wished to recognize such echoes and harmonies. But,
almost throughout the whole year, the Reading from the Old
Testament is specifically chosen because of its relationship
with the Gospel of the day; it clarifies the Gospel and is in
turn clarified by it.

Continuity between Two Testaments

However important these continuities of words and especially of themes between the two Testaments happen to be,
they are not the most important ones. There exists between
the Testaments a *real* continuity, that is, a continuity of realities and of events. There are not two plans of God, of
which the first was as it were a rough sketch which God then

rejected for the benefit of a more definitive plan. There is one single plan and design of God which goes from creation and Abraham to the final consummation passing through this decisive point, inaugurating "the end of the times" which is Jesus Christ.

Christianity is not a collection of frozen dogmas which have fallen from heaven totally fashioned. It is a history, from which the dogmas have issued by a sort of crystallization process, and by which God at one and the same time announces salvation and realizes it. We form part of this history, but so do Abraham, Moses, and David. They are not strangers with respect to us. They are our ancestors.

They have built the house in which we dwell; they have traced the road we follow; they have tended to the term we pursue. If, at Mass, we hear about their exploits, their adventures, their failures, it is not to satisfy an archeological or retrospective curiosity; this we have a perfect right not to appreciate. But it is because the Mass forms a part of a history, *our* history, of which they too form a part.

This is why during the Sundays of Lent, which makes us relive the history of salvation until the Passover of Christ that forms its culmination, the Readings from the Old Testament are chosen for a special reason. Their choice is based not on their precise relation to an individual Gospel but on their suitability in recalling five of the decisive stages of the history of salvation under the Old Law.

The Readings from the Old Testament are also chosen according to another principle during the time of Advent-Christmas-Epiphany; they are messianic prophecies. Some might say that these prophecies have been fulfilled in Jesus Christ and, therefore, can no longer interest us. This is not true! They have been fulfilled only in part by the First Advent or Coming which we no longer wait for, but they have to be fulfilled completely by the Second Coming, which we are still waiting for, so that the hope of the Prophets is still *our* hope.

This is why we say concerning the Holy Spirit in the Creed, "He spoke through the Prophets." The Prophets were waiting for a Messiah for Whom we no longer wait. They did not know *Who* that Messiah would be whose Name we know. But, in awaiting Him and in announcing Him, they teach us *what* that Messiah is, and they enable us to know Him better.

Christological Character of Both Testaments

What we have just said in more detail about the Prophets is true of the whole Old Testament, which is wholly prophetical, and completely Christological, that is, speaking about the Christ, the Messiah. This fact was recalled by the Risen Jesus to the disciples of Emmaus: "O foolish ones and slow of heart to believe in all that the Prophets have spoken! . . . And beginning then with Moses and with all the Prophets, He interpreted to them *in all the Scriptures* the things referring to Himself" (Lk 24, 25. 27). And to the Apostles Jesus said: "These are the words which I spoke to you while I was yet with you *that all things must be fulfilled that are written* in the Law of Moses and the Prophets and the Psalms *concerning Me*" (Lk 24, 44). This enumeration takes in the whole Old Testament.

In reality, since Jesus is the Word of God and therefore the Author of all Revelation, we must say that in these ancient Scriptures He is not merely spoken about by different authors, but it is *He Himself Who speaks,* Who still speaks to us today. As is stated in the *Constitution on the Sacred Liturgy* (art. 7): "Christ is always present in His Church, especially in her liturgical celebrations. . . . He is present in His word, since it is He Himself Who speaks when the Holy Scriptures are read in the Church" and this not only in Readings of the Gospel or the New Testament.

No doubt the Old Testament is imperfect. The morality it expresses, and especially the one which sacred history records as practiced, is sometimes still crude. We should not look upon this sketchy revelation as a finished product, as is sometimes done by certain sects which reproach Christians for having replaced the Jewish Sabbath with our Sunday. We know that this revelation is progressive, pedagogical, and that it has found its fulfillment only in Christ.

We must not fear that the Liturgy will "judaize" us; if it reads the Old Testament to us, it is within an ensemble of texts in which appear also the New Testament with the Acts of the Apostles, first history of the Church, the Epistles, the Apocalypse or Book of Revelation, and especially the Gospel. We do not want to separate the root and the stem from its flower and its fruit.

22. THE RESPONSORIAL PSALM

This psalm is well named. First, because of its structure. It is chanted normally by a small choir or a soloist, and the whole people, after each verse, repeats a simple and uniform *response* or refrain.

But there is a more profound reason: this name "responsorial" designates its functional role in the Liturgy of the Word. God is the first to speak to us, to interpellate us, and we respond by a Psalm chant.

Indeed, what better way to respond to the Word of God than by means of the Word of God? The whole Bible is the Word of God, hence so are the Psalms. But they are at the same time the Word of God in a form which enables us to use these words and address them to God. To them can be applied the wonderful formula used by God in relation to Jeremiah (1, 9): "See, I place *My* words in *your* mouth," thus defining his prophetic mission.

The Psalms are prophetic—like the rest of the Old Testament; but they are prophetic in a very special way, because they intensely express the hope and the prayer of Israel, they tend toward the coming of the Messiah. They are "Christo-

logical" in the sense that they speak of Christ but also in the
sense that in them it is Christ Who speaks to His Father. [25]
When we have understood this we are in the possession of
the key to the Psalms, we can relish the vigor of their "elan"
Godward, their profound authentic piety, their sense and
spirit of praise and of thanksgiving. There exists no more
beautiful school of prayer.

Some of the faithful are at first disturbed when they encounter the imprecations and maledictions so frequently
found in the Psalms, and which seem so foreign to the kindness found in the Gospels. Let us not exaggerate the difficulty. First of all, there is more than just kindness in the
Gospel. [26] On the other hand, the enemies against whom the
psalmist cast his imprecations—which are violent but soft-
enned by their conventional and stereotyped character—are
much less his personal enemies than enemies of God, whose
servant he is. Hence, we shall see in them only the enemies
of Christ and of His reign. Moreover, these passages which
sound somewhat painful are not used in the Mass.

Prolongation of Previous Reading

Since it is a prophecy, the Responsorial Psalm is not a
chant to fill in an interval, or to accompany a liturgical function by giving it a sonorous adornment, as is the case of the
Psalm which accompanies the entrance procession and the
Communion procession.

The Responsorial Psalm must be listened to for itself in a
spirit of recollection. It continues in a lyrical way the Reading

---

[25] These different aspects of the Christology of the Psalms form the
framework of our introductory volume on the Psalms: *Le Miel du
Rocher ou la douceur des Psaumes* [*Honey from the Rock or the Sweet-
ness of the Psalms*] Ed. du Cerf, 1967.

[26] Read for example chapter 23 of St. Matthew; read the maledictions (or woes) which counterbalance the Beatitudes in St. Luke 6,
24-25; the parable of the homicidal vine-dressers in the three synoptic
Gospels, for example in St. Luke 20, 9-19; in St. John 5, 37-47, and the
whole of chapter 8, as also 9, 39-41.

which has gone before and helps to assimilate this reading in prayer. It is for this reason that it has been chosen. Hence it is almost a fourth Reading. St. Augustine considered it this way and he usually took it as a theme for his homily, so much so that one day the bishop of Hippo had to improvise his homily because the cantor had made a mistake about the Psalm that had to be sung.

The best way, of course, is to place the Psalm between the first and the second Reading, whereas the "Acclamation" of the Gospel is another interlude between the Epistle and the Gospel. In this way one observes the alternation between the Psalms and the Readings that was already the rule followed in the synagogue.

However, if there are only two Readings, the Responsorial Psalm and the Acclamation of the Gospel follow each other immediately, between the two Readings. This was the practice of the Roman Church until very recently. But it is also permissible to choose one of the two intervenient chants.

If we omit the Reading taken from the Old Testament, what can be the meaning of the Responsorial Psalm, which, as we have pointed out, was chosen on account of its close relationship with it? It is not hard to solve this problem. The lyrical and Christological character of the Psalm will often allow it to be in harmony at least in a general way with the rest of the Mass and especially with the Gospel. If this is not the case, it is permissible to choose from a collection of Responsorial Psalms those which are adapted to the season of the year.

23. THE READING OF THE APOSTLE

The official documents of the Council for the restoration of the Liturgy now speak of the "Second Reading." The expression is not at all poetical and, besides, the term will be inexact if the First Reading is omitted: the "second" will then become the first!

The Roman Liturgy always used the term "Epistle" for the Reading which preceded the Gospel even when it was not taken from an Epistle but from a book of the Old Testament, the Acts of the Apostles, or the book of Revelation. The improper use of the term with its broadened meaning possibly constitutes a trace of the ancient custom of having three Readings, the second being actually a portion of an Epistle.

The Eastern liturgies call this Reading as well as the book in which it is found: "the Apostle." This title has the advantage of being suitable for all the books of the New Testament, the Epistles as well as the Acts and Revelation. [27]

However, it is not certain that the Epistle of James was authored by the Apostle of that name. Its author is the "brother," that is, cousin, of the Lord. Some identify the author with the Apostle James, son of Alpheus, also called James the Less. In any case, if the Epistles of James (and of Jude) have been accepted as canonical, that is "regular," containing the Word of God, it is because they came from the Church of the Apostles, sharing in the incomparable authority of those who had been the companions of Jesus, His witnesses who were then sent by the Lord Jesus and who had been charged with continuing His mission.

Meticulous spirits might remark that the Gospels themselves could rightly be called "(Reading of) the Apostle" since they set down the apostolic preaching. Two of the four evangelists did not belong to the Twelve, it is true, but St. Mark is the interpreter of Peter, according to a tradition which remains unshaken, and St. Luke says in his prologue that he has taken care to get his information from eyewitnesses (Lk 1, 2-3).

It is quite certain that the Gospels are not an instantaneous report of the actions and words of Jesus. These have been

---

[27] Some will object that neither Mark nor Luke were "apostles," properly so-called, but it is a fact that they have always been designated as such in the liturgical books. [Tr.]

arranged, rethought and deepened in the apostolic catechetical teaching. Nevertheless, in the Gospels, the Apostles are self-effacing in the presence of the Master.

Apostles Come before Us Today

On the contrary, in the other writings of the New Testament, the Apostles are either the principal personages, as in the Acts of the Apostles, or the Apostle who writes them comes to the fore and does not hesitate to speak in the first person: "I . . . an Apostle of Jesus Christ," "Paul, the servant of Jesus Christ, called to be an Apostle . . . grace be to you . . . first I give thanks. . . ." The title "Apostle" given to their writings is very evocative; it makes the person of the Apostle stand out, as it were, in the midst of the liturgical assembly to direct to us a preaching which is always actual, in the Church which we characterize in the Creed as "apostolic," meaning that the Apostles are its unshakable foundations (cf. Mt 15, 18; Eph 2, 20).

This Apostle addresses himself not only to his contemporaries who have disappeared so long ago from this earth; but through the Christians who lived in the first century in Rome, Corinth, Philippi, Colossae, or in the "dispersion" (cf. Jas 1, 1; 1 Pt 1, 1), it is to us, their fellow Christians of the 20th century, that the Apostle recalls the love of the Father in Jesus Christ, the folly of the Cross, the Good News of our redemption, the primordial duty of charity; it is we who are exhorted to imitate Christ, to shun divisions, etc.

On the principal feasts and major Sundays the passages from these Epistles have been chosen in accord with their relation to the Mystery celebrated. Sometimes it is not a question of making use of dispersed fragments but of a Reading that will be almost continuous. Thus, during the Christmas Season the first Epistle of St. John is read almost completely and successively, beginning on the very day of the feast of its author (December 27), since this Epistle is wholly dominated by the Mystery of love found in the Incarnation. In the Easter Season a very large part of the First Epistle of St. Peter is read because it deals at length with the grandeur of, and the demands originating from, our Baptism, which is a participation in the Paschal Mystery.

You may notice that on Sundays these passages of the Epistle, whether continuous or dispersed, are generally very short. These texts, after all, are so packed with meaning that a few verses suffice to provide very rich food for our meditation.

On weekdays during the 34 weeks of the "Season of the Year," longer fragments are read, for then it is a question of a "semi-continuous" reading which must enable us to know the Epistles if not in their entirety, at least in their principal parts and in their general unfolding.

People Need a Hand Lectionary

The majority of Christians do not attend Mass during the week. But those who do go constitute an elite which has a right to a choice fare. Besides it is to be hoped that all good Christians will buy a lectionary incorporated in a missal, or distinct from it, and one that is provided with notes and instructive introductions. They will thus possess a Biblical anthology that might be more attractive to them than a complete Bible, and it is greatly to be hoped that they read it frequently in private.

In that way the Lectionary will not be merely a liturgical book but a privileged instrument which will enable Christians who are sincerely desirous of strengthening and vivifying their faith, by studying its sources, to acquire a true Biblical culture. We do not mean the critical and profound science of Biblical specialists, but one similar to that which was possessed by Mary who "kept all these things carefully in her heart" (Lk 2, 51). Such assiduous contact with these profound texts will enrich them and renew their Christian spirit.

24. THE GOSPEL ACCLAMATION

The First Reading was followed by a Responsorial Psalm. After the Second Reading there is another chant but one that has a totally different character. The Responsorial Psalm was a meditation developed for its own sake, although it prolonged the preceding Reading. The chant that comes after the Second Reading is a short acclamation directed to the Reading which is to follow.

It accompanies the short procession of the Gospel: the priest or the deacon goes to fetch the Book, and before he goes to the ambo [28] to proclaim the Word, prays to God or asks the blessing of the priest who wishes him to read the sacred text not only "worthily" but so that the audience will truly receive the Good News: "Let him who has ears to hear, hear!"

The Acclamation honors Christ Who will come to "evangelize" us. No doubt, as we have recalled, it is "He Himself who speaks while the Holy Scriptures are read in the Church" *(Constitution on the Sacred Liturgy,* art. 7). But in the Gospel He will speak to us in a way that is much clearer, more personal, more decisive, and more enriching than in the texts which have come before.

This Acclamation enshrines a short Biblical sentence, praising Christ in His function of Teacher (Master), Revealer, or it recalls a scriptural axiom characteristic of the feast or the day. The people customarily make the Acclamation by the *Alleluia,* except during Lent when this Acclamation which is proper to the Easter Season is replaced by an equivalent formula.

---

[28] From the Greek *anabaino,* to mount: a high place from which the Word of God is proclaimed.

25. "THE GOSPEL OF JESUS CHRIST"

The fact that the reading of the Gospel enjoys a superior dignity is clearly shown by many of its liturgical features. It is the only Reading which is preceded by a procession, by an Acclamation, by a blessing and a prayer. It is reserved for the deacon, and in his absence, for the priest, whereas the other Readings can be proclaimed by clerics of a lower rank, by lay people, and in certain cases by women.

It is honored by lighted candles and incense. It is preceded by a call for attention: "The Lord be with you." At the beginning one makes the sign of the Cross. At the end the priest, or deacon, kisses the book—an act of loving homage evidently addressed to Christ Himself.

Finally, the people—beside the preliminary Acclamation —.responds by the acclamation: "Glory to You, Lord" when the title is announced, and still another acclamation at the end of the reading: "Praise to You, Lord Jesus Christ."

Let us come back to the announcement at the beginning. In official Latin books it is formulated thus: "A reading from the holy Gospel according to (Luke, Matthew, etc.)." Until recent times one said "Sequentia" i.e., "sequence" of the holy Gospel . . .; this suggested a continuous reading. Quite often this is not correct and, moreover, why reserve this mention of a "sequence" to the Gospel in contrast with the Epistles?

With respect to saying "A reading from the Gospel of John, or Luke . . ." this could lead some to think that each evangelist has recorded the Gospel according to his fancy. Perhaps "according to John, etc.," is a less misleading formula. All should remember one fact: there is but one only Good News, the one Jesus Christ has brought into the world.

It is interesting to note that Mark's Gospel begins thus: "The beginning of the Gospel of Jesus Christ, the Son of God." But, of course, it has been transmitted to us by four evangelists, each with his own style, temperament, perspective, and each having in mind different people to whom he addressed himself.

Will Help People Know Gospels Better

Now, how many Catholics are able to discern the characteristics of the four evangelists? There are some who think that the "Gospels" are only the short pieces read at Mass and they may not even know that these come from four small books, each constituting a unit which has its definite plan. Others, having perhaps read some years ago a popular harmony of the Gospels or one of those *Lives of Jesus Christ* which no exegete would wish to write today, imagine that the four Gospels are interchangeable.

The use of the new Lectionary (in handbook form or incorporated in a hand Missal), should do away with such ignorance. In fact, its cycle of three years consecrates more especially the year A to Matthew, the year B to Mark, and the year C to Luke. [29] And so, by listening a whole year to only one evangelist in preference to others, the people will be able to know him a little better and distinguish him from the others.

Matthew is more simple, more doctrinal (more ready to teach), more rich in discourses, more anxious to show that Jesus fulfills the prophecies of Scripture. Mark is shorter as to the ensemble, but more concrete in details, more attached to recounting miracles than reporting discourses, desirous to show the Messianic and Divine power of Jesus. Luke is a more elegant writer, anxious not to shock the pagans; he is the evangelist of Divine Mercy and of the joy of those who benefit from it, one who paints the portraits of women (Mary of Nazareth, Elizabeth, the sinner who was pardoned, the widow of Nain, Martha and Mary of Bethany in their home).

---

[29] It is easy to discern in what years particular Gospels appear. The years C are those whose numbers, in the thousand, when added, give a multiple of 3 (for example 1971, 1974, 1977). Those that precede them (1970, 1973, 1976) belong to the years B. Those that follow them (1972, 1975, 1978) belong to the years A.

The frequent use of the Lectionary will no doubt also make the attentive listener become aware of the "synoptic problem," [30] when he finds the same scene treated somewhat differently by different authors: for example, every year, when on the first and the second Sunday of Lent the episodes of the temptation of Christ in the desert and of the Transfiguration are presented.

The Gospel of St. John has no year proper to it. But it occupies a place suited to its great importance. The sixth chapter (on the Bread of Life) is found in year B consecrated to Mark (whose text would be too short to be used for a whole year) after his account of the multiplication of the loaves.

Three major episodes, which are proper to John and which tradition connects with the formation of candidates for baptism, are read on the third, the fourth, and the fifth Sunday of Lent during year A. [31] These three major episodes are: the conversation with the Samaritan woman (ch. 4), the cure of the man born blind (ch. 9), the resurrection of Lazarus (ch. 11).

His Prologue ("In the beginning was the Word") is read each year on Christmas Day; the apparition of the risen Jesus to the Apostles is read on the second Sunday of Easter (eight days after the feast) and on Pentecost Sunday; chapter 10, about the Good Shepherd, and finally the discourse after the Last Supper, on the last Sundays of Easter.

Will Help People Know Jesus Better

Be it well understood, that if we must pay attention to particularities of the style, methods, and aims of the dif-

---

[30] The synoptic problem concerns the problem of the mutual influences or the common origin of the first three evangelists. Sometimes the three are placed in parallel columns which brings out their common and their divergent parts.

[31] It will even be permissible to read them in other years in parishes or communities that prepare adults for Baptism.

ferent evangelists, it is not for the purpose of drawing delec-
tation from the exercise of literary criticism. The thing that
interests us in the Gospel is Jesus Christ, Who is at the same
time the One Who reveals and the Object of the revelation.

Yet if we read only one evangelist (it is this way that the
Roman Liturgy has for too long a time favored St. Matthew),
or if we consider the four evangelists as speaking the same
language, our vision of Jesus will lack depth. But when we
look at Him in turn through those four witnesses whose differences we have learned to appreciate, we get a vision of
Him which we may be allowed to call stereoscopic; then
those differences restore life and depth to our vision of our
Lord.

What helps us to contact Jesus in person, through the
evangelical accounts, is above all faith, the essential founda-
tion of the "active participation" in the Word and in the
Eucharist. It is faith which makes us reach Jesus as living,
as actual, as speaking to us today in His Gospel proclaimed
in the Church, in the Mass.

What we have said about the other Readings is still more
applicable to the Gospel. If the Old Testament ought to interest us because the people who lived it and the Prophets
who preached it are *our* people and proclaim what is still
our hope today, *a fortiori* the primitive community of the
disciples, who heard Jesus and have reported His Gospel
after preaching it, is *our* community: we are not mere audi-
tors of those ancient disciples; we are the disciples of today.

If the Apostle is alive among us when he speaks to us in
the Liturgy and challenges us through the Christians of
Corinth or of Rome, through Titus or Timothy, how much
more alive among us is Jesus Who, far superior to Isaiah or
to St. Paul, is going to offer Himself for us and with us on
the altar; how much more reason for realizing that He challenges us, He Who is, in contrast with all the Prophets and
all the Apostles, the interior Master or Teacher?

Related to this important teaching of the actuality of Jesus in the Gospel is a small problem concerning the way we ought to present and translate our *pericopes.* [32]

For many centuries, most of the passages of the Gospel read in the Roman Mass began with "At that time." [33] There are some specialists in the history of religions who attribute a great importance to "that time," seeing it as a "time" of special quality. But they also see in it a mythical time, that is, one that transcends our terrestrial time. [34]

But the 'time" of the Gospel is not a mythical time; it is a real, terrestrial time, even if the events that are recorded have a bearing far beyond the time of the actual happening. For most of our contemporaries the stereotype "at that time" [35] calls up either a distant past ("a very long time ago"), or a story that is something of a fable ("once upon a time").

And yet we cannot begin a story, report a discourse of Jesus or of an Apostle without first situating it in time, for otherwise it will sound non-temporal or fortuitous. On the other hand, it is a good thing for a reading to start with some preparatory words.

The "Consilium" which has established the official text of the Lectionary has tried, whenever possible, to replace what was banal and vague in "at that time" with something chronologically more definite, generally taken from the text

---

[32] This term comes from the Greek and means a portion *cut out.* In exegesis this word is used to designate the small literary units which can be discerned in a scriptural book, and in the Liturgy it indicates the text which will be read in particular circumstances, as is done during Mass.

[33] There were some exceptions, e.g., when the time was indicated in the beginning of the text: "In the fifteenth year of the reign of Tiberius . . ."; "Before the feast of the Passover . . .." etc.

[34] Cf. Mircea Eliade: *Historical Treatise of Religions,* Section 150: Restoration of the Mythical Time.

[35] The same is true of the expression "In those days" which traditionally opens the accounts of the Old Testament and the Acts of the Apostles. These have received a solution similar to the one that will be described for the Gospel.

itself. In this way the Biblical passages more closely resemble reports of real facts, situated in history. But our faith tells us that they are not shut up in a period of time long past; they really concern us TODAY.

26. THE HOMILY

We said a moment ago that the Scripture proclaimed at Mass is living and actual, that it concerns us. This actuality does not become immediately evident, for what we read or hear read are texts composed two thousand and more years ago. Most of the faithful, and not only those who have had little education, find the Bible strange, distant, and difficult.

These are true obstacles. But let us not exaggerate them! We have the means to lessen such difficulties.

Are we obliged to believe that the faithful are completely closed to the language of the Bible? And hence also to the language of faith? When we hear the remark, "They don't talk that way. It's something that doesn't belong to their vocabulary," must we not say to ourselves, that critic seems to know little about the life of a vocabulary in every human being? Does not everybody, in his childhood and throughout the whole course of his life, constantly encounter new terms, which he then assimilates without noticing it? If this were not a fact we should still be mumbling terms from our infancy, such as, "da-da," "ma-ma," etc.

Bible Texts Need to be Explained

Our Biblical and liturgical texts are reproached for using terms that are foreign to popular language. Yet any workman reading his newspaper or a mass-circulation magazine, or looking at television, sees and hears dozens of technical terms used in genetics, electronics, or astronautics which he assimilates at least in a confused fashion thanks to their context, so that he understands the general meaning of an article or a broadcast. These are terms he does not customarily use, but he knows full well that a technician is obliged to use special terms, and he himself uses such terms that belong to his trade or profession.

Let us add that the Bible, with very few exceptions, such as Paul's Epistle to the Ephesians, avoids abstract ideas; simple people feel more at home in it than intellectuals and semi-intellectuals who are more or less affected by "dualism" [36] and are accustomed to a deductive and rigorous way of reasoning.

If the faithful do not understand the Bible, it is not because they have never heard it explained. It is principally because they have never been put in assiduous and prolonged contact with Holy Scripture. To hold that we should wait before using the new Lectionary until we have given them a serious preparation for it is not to be taken seriously.

If we were to wait to give a child something to eat until we taught him the physiology of nutrition, he would starve to death. We learn a language by contact, by contagion. We get to know a poet by reading his poems, not critical studies about him.

The Lectionary gives the faithful a contact with most of the books of the Bible. [37] It offers them choice portions by eliminating those arid sections in which a good number of indiscriminate readers of the whole Bible get lost. The Lectionary underlines the harmony between the two Testaments

---

[36] Philosophical position (of the ancient Greek philosophers and later of men like Descartes) which separate soul and body into two distinct—if not opposite—complete substances. Biblical language knows only the concrete man and calls him either "flesh" or "soul." But we must note that when St. Paul speaks of the "flesh" as opposed to the "spirit" (but not to the soul), he then means by it human nature in its weakness and inclination to sin.

[37] Especially when also privately meditated on with the aid of hand Lectionary or hand Missal. [Tr.]

and highlights the major passages, reserving them for the principal feasts and the more important seasons of the liturgical year. Nothing is better suited to give the people of God the meaning of the Bible as well as a taste for it. This is the "direct" method.

No doubt, various ways of initiation can enable them to get a more thorough knowledge of the Bible. There are many books and reviews, and there are also study-clubs that can help persons at any level of culture to improve their Scriptural knowledge and appreciation.

Diverse editions of the Lectionary, destined for different categories of people, with introductions and more or less detailed notes, will most likely find a wider reading public. It is to be hoped that such books will habitually be given as presents at Christmas, on the occasion also of First Communion and a wedding, and that every Christian family will desire to have one.

Homily Provides Immediate Initiation

But it is also necessary to have an immediate initiation into the various texts that will be read in the assembly. This is precisely the role of monitions and the Homily.

The difference between these two sorts of commentaries is considerable. It does not consist merely in their different duration, as if a monition were only a short Homily, and the Homily a prolonged monition.

Their differences consist first of all in the fact that the monition *precedes* the Reading, but the Homily *follows* it. Secondly, the monition is solely didactic; it is content with awakening the mind, helping it to understand the meaning of the text that will be read, and the particular place it has in the Celebration; the Homily, on the contrary, starts from the texts that have been read and extends to the whole of life.

The monition is intended to *explain* the texts very briefly. The Homily wishes to *apply* them. Our Lord gave us an example of a Homily when, in the synagogue of Nazareth, He read a text from Isaiah: "The Spirit of the Lord is upon me . . ." (Lk 4, 16-30). It does not appear that He gave monitions explaining the text He was to read; after all, the text was well known by the hearers. With respect to His Homily, one might think first that He contented Himself with saying only this sentence: "Today this Scripture has been fulfilled in your hearing."

But Jesus must have developed this theme, of which Luke gives us merely the summary, for the evangelist afterward shows us the most vivid impression that was produced by what no doubt was a true discourse: "All bore Him witness and marveled at hearing the words of grace that came from His mouth." But the inhabitants of Nazareth were scandalized; they began to doubt for they now recalled that this prophet was their fellow citizen whom they had known in His infancy. [38]

Jesus answers them, "No prophet is acceptable in his own country"; and now comes the second part of His Homily: starting from events of the Old Testament, He shows God's kindness toward those strangers such as the widow of Zarephath and Naaman the Syrian; He opens to them the perspectives of a salvation which is not limited to their people, but is universal. There is no question here of an explanation of the text of Isaiah taken out of time and place but of an ardent application to the situation current at that time, one so brilliant that the people cast Him out of the synagogue and then from the town and attempt to throw Him down into a precipice.

This, we believe, is the way a Homily, if it wishes to be based on the Word of God, must apply this ancient Word, destined for all, to the present assembly here *today*. Hence,

---

[38] On this point, the parallels are more explicit (Mt 13, 55-57; Mk 6, 2-3).

the Homily belongs to the office of the celebrant and as much as possible to the pastor.

It is not a conference on Holy Scripture. It is a sacramental and pastoral act. Sacramental because it is in line with the Eucharistic Celebration, of which the proclamation of the Word forms a part. It is pastoral because it must flow out into the real and concrete life of the hearers.

The new Lectionary, since it offers a great variety of texts to the preacher, will enable him to renew himself, preventing him from becoming too repetitive and stale. But there are those who fear being immersed in such great wealth. This was the objection uttered at a Diocesan Convention of Priests (see pp. 66-67). Here is what was answered by experts:

> "As regards the Homily, we must avoid desiring to *say everything* and *explain everything;* neither must we try to *make a synthesis* of all the Readings. Ordinarily, there is an inter-relation between the text of the Old Testament and the Gospel, but the Second Reading is not necessarily in harmony with the others. Hence, we must not force our imagination to go through circus stunts in order to discover some synthesis at any price."

Let us stop for a moment and have a look at that word *Homily*. It has been placed again in an honorable position by the Council's *Constitution on the Sacred Liturgy,* which gives us an excellent definition of it: "By means of the Homily the Mysteries of the Faith and the guiding principles of the Christian life are expounded from the sacred text during the course of the liturgical year. The Homily, therefore, is to be highly esteemed as part of the Liturgy itself" (art. 52).

Homily Is a "Familiar Talk"

In some quarters this word had acquired a "bad name" because it suggested a moralizing and boring kind of sermon. It comes from the Greek *homilia* which designates a familiar talk. "Talk" does not mean it must be a "dialogue"; and "familiar" does not mean it must border on the common.

A Homily is an act of the celebrant in his official capacity. But it differs from more solemn forms of oratory, as might still be heard at the ordination of a bishop. It is "familiar," one might say, in the sense of being addressed to a family—which is true of the audience the priest addresses; "father" distributes the "daily bread" to his spiritual children, the "pastor," to the members of his flock, making sure they have good food and enough.

The Homily deserves its name of "familiar talk," if the pastor, who knows his "sheep" very well from daily contact with them, answers in his monologue the real questions that the parishioners ask themselves. This he does, "starting from the sacred text," because his authority flows from that of the Word of God.

He does not desire to give a complete explanation of this Word, let us repeat once more, but simply strives to make the Word better understood, to actualize it, to apply it to particular needs and situations of the moment. The Homily starts from the Word of God, but it starts also from life; these two must be brought together, they must explain and vivify one another.

To the extent that the preacher is profoundly impregnated with the Word of God through study, meditation, and prayer, and that he truly shares, through pastoral charity, the concerns of his parishioners, his Homily *is* the Word of God, less strictly of course than the proclamation of the inspired Word, but in a way derived from it yet no less real.

And since "it is part of the Liturgy itself" it pertains to the progression of the Liturgy of the Word, if it does not content itself with being a classroom instruction or a professorial explanation. It must aim at *converting* the People of God— (as in a few minutes the Word of Christ will *convert* the bread and wine into the Body and Blood of Christ)—changing that People into a holy people, better prepared to offer the Eucharist and to offer themselves with the High Priest and Victim. More than a lesson, it is a preparation and an exhortation for a commitment of charity which is demanded by the Eucharist.

27. THE CREED

The Liturgy of the Word ends with the recitation of the Creed and the dialogued litany of the Universal Prayer, better known as the Prayer of the Faithful.

It is here especially that we see the inadequacy of the old term "Mass of the Catechumens," for the Creed was introduced into the Roman Mass only in the 11th century, and the discipline of the catechumenate had been abolished or fallen into desuetude already for a long time. This discipline consisted in *dismissal* (missa) of the catechumens at the end of the Liturgy of the Word. The Prayer of the Faithful then followed because it was reserved for those who were baptized.

Why did the liturgical mind of the Roman Church so long oppose the introduction of the Creed into the Mass? For the simple reason that it is the "Symbol of Faith," in other words, the sign by which believers are able to recognize one another,[39] and that sign belonged to the initiation Sacrament of Baptism.

The Creed, or Symbol of Faith, is merely a development of the three questions concerning faith in the three Divine Persons which were addressed to the candidates for Baptism and their threefold answer: "I believe." This for a long time was the "form" of Baptism.

But there is a more profound reason for this opposition. It was felt that the recitation of the Creed at Mass was as it

---

[39] It may be useful to recall here that the word symbol (*sunbolon*) comes from the Greek *sunballein*, a picturesque word signifying to bring together, re-encounter; and that a symbol or sign of mutual recognition consisted of some object which had been broken into two parts. When these were brought together, for instance, by people who had not seen one another for a long time, the fitting union of the two parts served as a means of mutual recognition.

were duplicating the Mass itself, for its celebration is already a profession of faith: "As often as you eat this Bread and drink the Cup, you proclaim the death of the Lord until He comes" (1 Cor 11, 26).

Summary of Salvation History

The Creed is not a simple enumeration of articles of Faith, nor a summary of dogmatic teaching; it is a summary of the whole of salvation history, from Creation to Eternal Life, including the Incarnation, the Coming of the Holy Spirit, the Mystery of the Church and the Sacraments. It is a reminder of the economy of salvation, including the Mass.

It is in this sense that the Mass is called "the Mystery of Faith." If it is not so evident in the Roman Canon, it is clearly manifested in the new Eucharistic Prayers. The fourth one in particular retraces in so many details the stages of the history of salvation that it seems truly to duplicate the recitation of the Creed.

In spite of this the Church has retained the Creed in the Mass, at least on Sundays and other feast days when there was a greater assembly of the faithful. We shall therefore recite it willingly. We say recite, for it is more normal to recite a profession of faith than to sing it, unless it be a very simple recitative, as is the case of the Our Father which is another sign of recognition among the baptized.

We shall love this recitation of the Creed for a twofold reason. It constitutes a response to the Gospel. After hearing Christ speaking to us, we express our steady attachment to His message. At the same time, this recitation recalls our privilege as baptized persons. Not only does Baptism make us members of the priestly and royal people and enable us to participate in the Mass by offering it with the priest, but it has consecrated us as victims with Christ by associating us with His mystery of Death and Resurrection (cf. Rom 6, 3-11); it has consecrated us to the service and to the glory of the Father, and the Son, and the Holy Spirit. [40]

28. THE UNIVERSAL PRAYER
OR PRAYER OF THE FAITHFUL

Let us begin by answering an objection which could be made against the Universal Prayer, in the name of the principle of liturgical restoration which we have often mentioned and now recall once more: to avoid the repetitions at Mass which obscure the meaning and the inter-relation of the rites. The Universal Prayer, it is objected, duplicates the "Lord, have mercy" as well as the Commemorations of the Canon.

As we have said above, the "Lord, have mercy" is a vestigial remainder of a litany, and it is precisely this litany that one has desired to restore by instituting the Universal Prayer. But the "duplication" here is very negligible. If "Lord, have mercy" is incorporated in the Penitential Rite (Confiteor), preserving it here is justified because it has a new function.

In regard to the Commemorations, let us remember first of all that the twofold Commemoration, for the living and the dead, exists only in the Roman Canon. But one may use a special prayer for this or that deceased person in Eucharistic Prayer II and III. In these different cases, there is question of *this* living person or *this* deceased person designated by the letter N. (which is an invitation to pronounce his or her *name*). It is a "particular intention." In the Universal Prayer there are only universal intentions. If the living or the dead are prayed for, it is only as belonging to a rather large category.

---

[40] Such, indeed, is the true meaning of the last command Christ gave to His Apostles (Mt 28, 19) : ". . . . baptizing them in the name of the Father, and of the Son, and of the Holy Spirit." "In the name" does not mean here "by the authority of" but "*for* the name," that is, for the glory of the three Persons.

The term *"Universal Prayer"* is well chosen to indicate the characteristics of this litany. It is universal in its participants, it is universal in its objects.

It is universal because it is the affair of all the baptized who are present. Naturally, it is the principal celebrant who opens the Prayer and concludes it. Naturally, again, it is he, or another priest, or a deacon, a lector or a commentator, who expresses the intentions. But this is only the framework.

The substance of the Universal Prayer resides in the very simple invocations which all, clerics and lay people, have to express. The fact that a number of the faithful still remain mute in our churches indicates that not all have understood the importance of this prayer which gives them the opportunity to exercise their universal priesthood as baptized persons.

Four Series of Intentions

This prayer is also universal in the objects of its petitions. Left to ourselves, we often limit ourselves to petitions that are so selfish, so self-interested, so petty! As members of the universal Church, of which our small assembly is the visible and efficacious sign (the sacrament), we must pray for the universal interests of the Church: for the union of Christians, for the missions, for vocations, and for all the apostolic intentions that are those of the Pope, the College of Bishops, our bishop. [41] This then is the first category of the four series of intentions which must figure in the Universal Prayer if we want it to deserve the name.

The fourth of these intentions is restricted to the community which is present, but not in as much as it comprises such or such an individual; rather in as much as it is effectively (and this it should become more and more) a community which has the charge, as such, of rendering testimony to Christ and to His Gospel.

---

[41] Rather than for individual persons, who will be the explicit object of the prayer of the Church in the diverse Eucharistic Prayers where one must pronounce the names (N.) of the Pope and of the Bishop.

The other intentions make us look beyond the Church herself. The second concerns major temporal interests: those who govern, peace, the well-being of nations, freedom, and the progress of men. This transcends the Church and yet concerns it. St. Paul said it in a famous text to which we justly relate the institution of the Universal Prayer: [42] "I urge therefore, first of all, that supplications, prayers, intercessions and thanksgiving be made for all men; for kings, and for all in high positions, that we may lead a quiet and peaceful life in all piety and worthy behavior. This is good and agreeable in the sight of God our Savior, Who wishes *all men to be saved* and to come to the knowledge of the truth."

If "the Church is in Christ like a Sacrament or as a sign and instrument both of a very closely knit union with God and of the unity of the whole human race," [43] if "the Church . . . exists in the world, living and acting with it," and if "she goes forward together with humanity and experiences the same earthly lot which the world does [and] . . . serves as a leaven and as a kind of soul for human society," [44] it is normal for her to be interested in all great human causes.

There is, finally, the third of the great intentions of the Universal Prayer which, like the preceding one, goes beyond the frontiers of the Church; we pray for all who suffer: individuals, families, and nations, the poor and underdeveloped, the ignorant, the sick, the exiled, prisoners, the dying, the deceased, etc.

Sometimes the reproach is made that the Liturgy is hieratic, abstract, divorced from time. Certainly, it is before all the celebration of the Mystery of Christ, of the Paschal Mystery, which is situated in history and causes history to advance, but which necessarily expresses itself in Biblical terms, or terms sufficiently general so as to be suitable for all.

---

[42] 1 Tm 2, 1-4: cited in the *Constitution on the Sacred Liturgy,* art. 53.

[43] *Dogmatic Constitution on the Church,* art. 1.

[44] *Pastoral Constitution on the Church in the Modern World,* art. 40, par 2.

Nevertheless, this great prayer, this re-presentation of the Paschal Mystery which we call the liturgy, is connected with all of man's cares, ambitions, and miseries. And there are two moments in the Liturgy which, without constituting parentheses or being foreign to the Liturgy itself, show that it is interested in every man in what is most concrete and most actual: these are the Homily and the Universal Prayer.

It is not necessary for them to assume journalistic actuality or engage in polemics. They should not divide Christians. But they must open them to all human realities. That is why without seeking to transform the Mass into a sort of systematic demonstration, based on a theme, which would be to disfigure its "Mystery"-filled and poetic nature, it can be a good thing for the homilist to introduce into the Universal Prayer a particular intention which will transform into prayer the perspectives he has opened up by his preaching.

Thus ends the Liturgy of the Word. It has invited Christians not only to receive the revealed Truth but to take part in the combat for the coming of the Kingdom. In this way, it provides an immediate preparation for them to enter into the sacrifice not as spectators but as cooperators who will be able to offer and offer themselves with Christ for all their brothers.

THE LITURGY OF THE EUCHARIST

IV
THE PRESENTATION OF THE GIFTS

29. GOD'S BLESSING FOR THE BREAD AND WINE

The Liturgy of the Word is over. The People of God have been enlightened, nourished, vivified by this living word which inserts them into the plan of salvation. They have responded to it by chanting Psalms, Acclamations, or by meditating silently on the Divine Word, by listening to and assimilating the Word explained and applied in the Homily, and finally by professing their faith, in the Creed. But this is not enough.

The Word of God is not only an intellectual revelation, the transmission of truth. It is an action, it is the expression of a love which realizes and effects things; it carries man along in a plan of salvation which is a history. Hence, it is necessary for man to respond to it in turn by an action: this will be the *Eucharistic* action and sacrifice.

It is proper for us to respond to God's gift to us by a gift of our own, by a sacrifice which manifests our *gratitude* for His gifts. This already shows, and we must never forget it, that "thanksgiving" *(gratias agere)* means something quite different from a simple "thank you." Such a "thank you" is a limited act that corresponds to a particular gift. But God's gifts are all-inclusive; they embrace all that we have and all that we are: "What have you that you have not received?" (1 Cor 4, 7). Hence, to acknowledge this, to be grateful for them, will also be an all-inclusive action, without limit or restriction.

This action will consist in the Sacrifice of Christ, realized under the "species" (the visible forms) of the Eucharistic Sacrifice. This Sacrifice will be accomplished starting from bread and wine. The priest will begin, therefore, by taking bread and wine, as Jesus did: "on the night in which He was betrayed [He] took bread . . ." (1 Cor 11, 23; Mt 26, 26 and parallels).

This first phase, or rather, this preparation for the Sacrifice, is currently called "Offertory." Yet this seems to us to be a word we should do better to avoid. In itself it is wholly acceptable, for *offerre*, which gives our term "Offertory," can mean simply "to present," and at the moment this is all that is happening.

But *offerre* can also mean something much stronger and, one might say, more technical: it can signify "to offer" and even to "offer in sacrifice, to immolate." And we have not yet reached this point in the Mass. Moreover, if the words have any meaning, we cannot immolate bread and wine. The Mass is certainly an offering, but it is the offering of Christ. This takes place under the forms or appearances of bread and wine, evidently, but it is not bread and wine that are the victim of sacrifice.

Floods of ink and of words have been poured out, and much obscurity, regarding the first part of the Eucharistic Action when people have tried to explain it as an offering. Is it a first offering (of the bread and the wine) which precedes the one only true offering (of Christ)? Or is it simply an anticipation—but of the whole sacrifice—because one sees already in this bread and wine the Body and Blood of Christ which they will become?

We shall not lose our time in subtle discussions. We shall content ourselves with describing the rite of the preparation of the gifts as is required by the renewed Mass liturgy. This will be much more positive and hence much clearer.

Procession and Offertory Song

The rite may begin, if the Mass is sung, with the "Offertory Song." This is a fragment of a Psalm which only rarely expresses the idea of an offering. Originally, this chant accompanied the procession in which the gifts were brought to the altar. Its principal purpose was to create an atmosphere of joy, generosity, and praise in which this donation should take place.

Certainly, it is an excellent thing for the faithful, or for some who represent them, to bring their gifts: the bread and the wine destined for the Sacrifice, but also other offerings for the upkeep of the church edifice and for the clergy, for the relief of the poor. In this way, the participation of all is expressed.

But this procession has only the value of an expression. It is not essential. In the beginning of the liturgical renewal its importance has sometimes been exaggerated. And it has also been carried out in a mistaken and blundering fashion. For example, by having tools brought to the sanctuary, which cannot be "offered," since they will be taken back; they can only be blest; and such a blessing is only indirectly connected with the Mass.

In some places great importance has been attached to the "offering" of hosts, forgetting that such an "offering," which can help to count the number of communicants and has a certain symbolic value, in reality consists only in making hosts pass from one receptacle to another, since the present rules do not allow the priest to consecrate ordinary bread which the faithful might have brought from their homes.

It is at this time, in any case, that one places on the altar, which until now should have been empty, the corporal (cloth), purificator (napkin), chalice, and finally the Missal which will enable the priest to read the prayers which accompany this action.

The priest has ascended to the altar, for the first time since he kissed it at the beginning of the service. From a server he receives the paten with the bread. An explanation is needed here, for "paten" means a plate and in fact the paten was for a long time a small flat plate, because on it was placed only the large host of the priest.

Today, it is proper for the paten to be hollow or deep, like a soup plate or, better, a cup without a base, so that all "the bread" can be put in it: not only the host of the presiding priest, but the hosts of the other celebrants and of the people. For we shall see, when we study the Communion rite, that priests and faithful participate in the same Communion, in the same Sacrifice. Hence, it is not proper to place the hosts of the faithful apart, in a "ciborium." This vessel, which originally was merely a chalice with a cover and which by its shape seems to be a second chalice, ought to serve only for the reservation of hosts in the tabernacle.

Offering Bread and Wine

The priest elevates the paten with the bread a little before him, while pronouncing the formula:

> Blessed are You, Lord, God of all creation.
> Through Your goodness we have received this bread to offer,
> which earth has given and human hands have made.
> It will become for us the Bread of Life.

After this the priest performs a similar action, slightly elevating the chalice filled with wine and a little water, while pronouncing a parallel formula:

> Blessed are You, Lord, God of all creation.
> Through Your goodness we have received this wine to offer,
> fruit of the vine and work of human hands.
> It will become our Spiritual Drink.

This twofold formula is very noteworthy and we should consider it for a moment.

It is noteworthy first by its origin. It comes from the Jewish liturgy of repasts, especially of solemn banquets of confraternities, and of the Paschal supper. [1] This reminds us of the fact that the Christian Supper was grafted on the Jewish liturgy of repasts, which Jesus celebrated with His disciples on Holy Thursday evening.

It is a *berakah*, that is, a benediction or blessing. But here we must be on our guard against a misunderstanding. In our current religious language we understand "blessing" in the sense of a descent of the divine power on an object which it sanctifies in a more or less passing fashion. It is in this sense that today we speak of the blessing of meals, of houses, of a boat, or also of a blessing which will give a permanent kind of power to an object of piety such as altar cloths, rosary beads, or a medal.

In Biblical language, the blessing does not descend; it ascends. It is addressed to God to thank Him, one might almost say to congratulate Him, for His holiness, His greatness, and His gifts. Such a blessing is often pronounced in connection with some object, but then it is not the object which is blest, but God Who is "blest" in connection with this object. [2]

In this sense, benediction ("good word," in Greek *eulogia*) is almost synonymous with thanksgiving ("saying grace" after meals, *eucharistia* in Greek). Moreover, we notice that the Gospel uses these two words indifferently for one another in the account of the multiplication of the loaves and in that of the institution of the Eucharist. [3]

---

[1] Cf. Louis Bouyer, *L'Eucharistie*, ch. 4: "*Les* Berakoth *juives*," p. 83.

[2] Cf the Divine Praises ("Blessed be God . . .") at the end of the Benediction of the Blessed Sacrament. [Tr.]

[3] In the account of the first multiplication of the loaves, Jesus *blesses* in Mt 14, 19; Mk 6, 41; Lk 9, 16; and He *gives thanks* in Jn 6, 11. In

We bless God for the gift of bread, for He is the Creator of all things; all that is good and that sustains our life comes from His bounty. But the ancient Jews had such a strong sense of God's power that they neglected the human and even the cosmic intermediaries: it is God Who gives health and sickness, Who causes the rain to fall and the wind to blow.

Although God the Creator causes the wheat to sprout and the vine to grow, it is not He Who makes the bread and the wine, but man who by his labor adds to the work of God and transforms it. To note this is not to take anything away from God, for He has created man to His image and charged him to exercise dominion over His creation and perfect it.

Action of God and of Man

Hence, the liturgical formula under study mentions, besides the creative action of God, the constructive action of man. For this also we must bless God. And so the gifts we present to Him involve not only His goodness, but the work, intelligence, and collaboration of His children.

It is fitting that from the beginning of the Eucharistic Action we keep before our mind—and present to God while blessing Him for it—the fraternal labor of all humanity. By this we can already realize that in eating this bread and drinking this wine we shall unite ourselves not only with God but with our brothers. For though our faith assures us that this bread and this wine will be changed, through the consecration, into the Body and Blood of Christ, they do not

----

the accounts of the second multiplication of the loaves, Jesus *gives thanks* for the loaves in Mt 15, 36; Mk 8, 6; but He *blesses* the fishes in Mk 8, 7. At the Last Supper, Jesus *blesses* the bread in Matthew and Mark, while He *gives thanks* in Luke and Paul (1 Cor 11, 24), but He *gives thanks* over the cup in Matthew and Mark).

on that account lose their external features which remind us of their origin.

But in presenting this bread and this wine, which are still only bread and wine "of the earth," we already know what they will become: the "Bread of Life," and "our Spiritual Drink." Besides, the priest places them on the altar, the place of sacrifice, which represents Jesus Christ, Priest and Victim, Mediator of the Sacrifice.

This simple preparation of the gifts thus opens out to a sacrificial perspective. But it does not belong to the sacrifice, and it is not an offering in the strong sense of the word. We do not yet ask God to sanctify the gifts. We foresee that they will *become* [4] something else, something sublime and profitable for our spiritual life, but we are not asking this now.

This is the simple preparation of the gifts: the real offering and the epiclesis (invocation asking for the consecration) will take place only at the heart of the eucharistic prayer.

The two formulas we have studied are said in a low voice by the principal celebrant if at this time an Offertory Song or an equivalent canticle is sung. Otherwise, the priest may say these formulas in a loud voice, so that the faithful can participate in the "blessing" which the celebrant addresses to God; they do so by saying the acclamation: "Blessed be God for ever," after each formula.

30. THE PRESENTATION OF THE GIFTS (END)

The Preparation of the Chalice

We must now go back a little. The chalice has to be prepared, that is, wine must be poured into it, before the priest presents the chalice. This action belongs to the priest or to the deacon. It may be done at the credence table. For it is

---

[4] The Latin text says *fiet* which is a future; it does not read *fiat* which is a subjunctive. *Fiat* and *fiant* are found in the four Eucharistic prayers only in the prayer immediately preceding the Consecration.

important, especially when the altar faces the people, not to let the utilitarian manipulations that precede or follow the Eucharistic Liturgy, take on the same importance in the eyes of the faithful as sacred actions.

A little water is added to the wine. This was customary in our Lord's time, not only among the Jews, but also among the Greeks and the Romans, and it was done for a practical reason: the wine of the ancients was very heavy and very heady, and one could drink it only after greatly diluting it with water. But very soon, this utilitarian action took on a symbolic meaning and value. It is already known in the 2nd century, [5] in the 3rd century St. Cyprian will explain it as an important teaching, [6] and it will remain traditional. Water, the Book of Revelation tells us, represents the peoples (Rv 17, 15). Hence, this mingling has been looked upon as signifying the union in Christ of the Divine nature and the human nature. [7]

Modern interpretations that the "drop of water" represents *my* poor little personality, lost in the Sacrifice of Christ, in reality introduce a cloying element of the individual and the sentimental into the great and beautiful theme of the Mystery of the Redemption and of the Church.

In mixing water and wine, the priest has for a long time been saying, in the Roman Liturgy, a prayer composed by Pope St. Leo for the Prayer over the Gifts of Christmas and celebrating the union of the two natures in Christ. It had been adapted to its new use by being prefixed with the words: "By the Mystery of this water and wine." It is clear that the act of mingling water and wine is not mysterious at all, but it is the ritual evocation of a Mystery, namely, the

---

[5] St. Justin, *Apology* I, 65, 67.

[6] Letter 63 to Caecilius.

[7] This is why the Armenians who said that Christ had only the Divine nature (*phusis,* in Greek)—and are accordingly called Monophysites—did not put water in the chalice.

Incarnation. We ask that, as Christ became man, we ourselves might be divinized; this will be one of the effects of
the Sacrifice and of Communion. [8]

The Prayer of Azariah

After placing the chalice on the altar, the priest bows
down and says a prayer taken verbatim from the Book of
Daniel (3, 39-40). Here is a translation of this Biblical prayer,
in which we give in parentheses the words omitted by the
Liturgy, and in brackets those added:

> [Lord God], we ask You to receive us
> (as though it were holocausts of rams and bullocks or
>   thousands of fat lambs;)
> and be pleased with the sacrifice we offer You
> with humble and contrite hearts.

This Biblical book places the prayer on the lips of Azariah,
companion of Daniel, the young Jew who had been deported
to Babylon. Far away from the Temple which had been destroyed, he missed the solemn and bloody liturgies once
enacted there, but he understood that what pleases God first
of all is the spiritual sacrifice.

This thought is repeatedly found in Biblical piety, for example, in Hosea (6, 6):

> It is love that I desire, not sacrifice,
>   and knowledge of God rather than holocausts.

---

[8] This prayer has now been shortened by the suppression of the introductory and concluding words with respect to the text that formed
part of the Roman Missal for a thousand years. The essential thought
has been preserved. But by suppressing the principal proposition, "God,
grant us," we seem to make of the "mystery of this water and wine"
the very cause of our divinization. In the previous text, one was content to ask this of God "through the mystery of . . ." that is, basing our
petition on this gesture which calls up the Mystery of the Incarnation.
It would seem that it might have been better to keep the "God, grant
us" of the ancient text.

In Psalm 50 God rejects the bloody sacrifices not motivated
by a pure and religious intention. Finally, the conclusion of
Psalm 51 (vv. 18-19) reproduces the very terms of the prayer
of Azariah:

> For You are not pleased with sacrifices;
>   should I offer a holocaust, You would not accept it.
> My sacrifice, O God, is a contrite spirit;
>   a heart contrite and humbled, O God, You will not spurn.

At the very moment at Mass when the *matter* of the sacrifice is placed on the altar, it is good for us to remind ourselves that a material sacrifice is valueless if it does not express a sincere desire to renounce evil and to be united with
God. The "spiritual sacrifice" is not a disincarnate sacrifice;
it is truly a visible, concrete sacrifice, but one that is animated and rendered valuable by a total loving obedience.

St. Paul says in the same sense: "I exhort you, brethren,
by the mercy of God, to offer [present] your bodies [that is
your concrete person, your whole life] as a sacrifice, living,
holy, pleasing to God—your spiritual sacrifice [that is: in
this consists the spiritual worship you must render] (Rom
12, 1. 3).

The Incensation

The priest may then incense the gifts and the altar; this
is an optional rite and one now performed without words.
The perfume which is consumed by burning and sends its
smoke heavenward is an easily understood symbol of prayer
which must envelop, sanctify, and as it were spiritualize the
sacrifice. [8]

Then the deacon or a minister incenses the priest and the
people; this signifies that the people may not be separated
from their gifts, that they must offer themselves with them
and accompany them with their prayers.

---

[8] Cf. Ps 141, 2; Rv 5, 8; 8, 3-4.

The Washing of the Hands

The washing of the hands has been preserved at this place because the priest might have soiled his fingers when receiving the gifts or handling the censer. But this is really a symbolic purification which exists in all rites at different places, before an important action is begun.

While washing his hands, the priest underlines the spiritual character of this act, the requirement of purity imposed on the minister of the Eucharist, by saying the fourth verse of the *Miserere* (Ps 51):

[Lord,] wash away my iniquity;
cleanse me from my sin.

Pray, Brethren

This prayer, it must be confessed, is now superfluous, and we cannot help regretting that it has been retained by the authorities who exercise the final influence with respect to liturgical reform; they must have been swayed more by the desire not to disturb pious habits than to seek objectively to establish that clarity in the interconnection of rites which the Conciliar *Constitution* has set down as a major norm in the liturgical restoration.

I hope I shall be pardoned for making an allusion here to a personal trait. At a time when I had nourished the desire for some time that the *Orate, Fratres* (the Pray, brethren), should be suppressed, I found the picture souvenir of my priestly ordination which took place in 1933. On the back of the holy card I had chosen to print precisely the translation of the *Orate* (for at that time it was said in Latin, in a low voice and the server was the only one who responded to it).

In addition, my first sermon had been a paraphrase of the *Orate, Fratres.* For it then seemed very important to reveal to the faithful what the liturgical practice of the time and the current teaching did not permit them even to suspect: namely, that the Sacrifice which they regarded as an act proper to the priest was also their Sacrifice; hence their prayer, instead of running off aimlessly or turning back upon their own concerns, ought rather to be united with that of the principal celebrant.

At the beginning of the liturgical renewal, the *Orate, Fratres* had taken on great importance. Not only did it remind the faithful of the doctrine of active participation in the Liturgy, but it also gave them an opportunity to practice it. In the course of a Mass that was all in Latin, after a silent Offertory (sometimes entirely accompanied by music from the organ), before the Prayer over the Gifts said in a low voice (after all, was it not called the "Secret"), the faithful were happy to hear themselves addressed somewhat directly by the priest and to respond to him in a moderate voice.

But today the whole Mass is intelligible. The prayers accompanying the preparation of the gifts (or offerings) may now be said in an intelligible voice and call forth a response on the part of the faithful. The people have participated in the Universal Prayer, they will sing the "Holy, holy, holy," they will hear and understand the whole Eucharistic Prayer, participate in it by the acclamation of the anamnesis and conclude it with their amen.

Is it not superfluous, therefore, to invite them to participate, that is, to express by words what they are already doing in reality? To our mind, we have here a reduplication of the sort that the liturgical restoration asked us to suppress.

This is a phenomenon which sociologists call "a survival" [9] and biologists a "vestigial organ." May it at least cause younger people to suspect that before arriving at the present stage of the Liturgy, and at that participation of the people which appears so normal to them, a long journey was neces-

---

[9] They apply this name to an institution or a custom which maintains itself as it were through inertia after the reason for its existence has disappeared.

sary. For in the not too distant past, the priest had to declare to the faithful, against all appearances: "My Sacrifice, my brethren, is also your Sacrifice!"

31. THE PRAYER OVER THE GIFTS

The Introductory Rites of the Mass concluded with a Prayer, the Collect, which was immediately followed by the Liturgy of the Word. Likewise, the Offertory Rites end with a Prayer over the Gifts (or offerings), which is immediately followed by the Eucharistic Prayer.

It is not without purpose that we have just now used the term "offertory" which we had previously avoided. For it is the proper role of the Prayer over the Gifts to make us pass from a simple presentation of bread and wine to their being offered in view of the now explicit and approaching Eucharistic Sacrifice.

The true name of this Prayer, in Rome and from the beginning, was "Prayer over the (Gifts) presented" *(Oratio super oblata)*. Later, under the influence of the Gallican Liturgy, it came to be called the "Secret," no doubt because it had become the custom to say it, like the Canon which it sometimes anticipated, *secreto,* in a low voice. [10] From the time that it has been directed to be said aloud or sung [11]—as is logical for a Prayer—it has re-acquired its true name.

Recommends Gifts to God

What is its content? In it the priest explicitly presents to God the matter destined for the Eucharist. It is called gifts, presents, offerings: *dona, munera, oblata.* Up to now they are in fact only our gifts. But we know their final destiny. On

---

[10] A good number of other explanations have been given for this name "Secret." They are all hypothetical and arbitrary. The one we have given is the most probable one.

[11] First Instruction on the liturgical reform, *Inter Oecumenici,* of Sept. 26, 1964, art. 48 e.

this account they are called *oblata* or even *sacrificia:* an offering for the sacrifice.

These gifts are recommended to God; we are frequently
reminded that they are accompanied by prayers, that they
are the expression of the religious and zealous devotedness
(devotio) of His people, of His family. On great feasts, it is
stated that the object of the feast gives the Eucharist as it
were a special tonality. On feasts of Saints, there is a frequent petition that the intercession of the Saint may back
up our offering.

When we reflect upon it, this is perfectly admissible: poor
people that we are, we can only humbly present our modest
offering, and we must be supported by the intercession of
our glorious brothers in heaven. Nevertheless, many Secrets
in honor of the Saints cause us some embarrassment. It
seems sometimes that the Eucharistic Sacrifice would be offered in honor of a Saint more than to the glory of the Only
"Saint," and, as we know well that the gifts presented
by us will become the Body and the Blood of Christ, we feel
some discomfort when we have to say that our oblation, in
order to be pleasing to God, needs the reinforcement of a human prayer.

The Prayer over the Gifts, in this respect, is quite different
from the Collect. The latter is specific; it characterizes the
Mystery of the day or the liturgical season during which it
is said. The Prayer over the Gifts is functional, in the sense
that it fulfills a proper function in the structure of the Eucharistic Action. Hence, unlike the Collect, it needs not to be
particularized by the feast.

That is why the rigid rule that has linked the three Prayers
of the Mass has been relaxed. Frequently, with a Collect that
is proper and expresses the theme of the feast or the celebration of the Saint, a Prayer over the Gifts will be said which
is "common" in the sense that it will have a purely eucharistic purpose valid for any Mass.

Rooted in the Bible

What do we ask God in the Prayer over the Gifts? Simply, most of the time, that the gifts may please Him, that He may accept them benevolently. This theme may seem abstract and formalistic to us. Indeed, it is very much in line with the judicial spirit of the Latins, and we find it once more from one end to the other in the Roman Canon. However, it can justly claim to be rooted in the Bible [12] and to have a deep religious intention.

We are poor creatures, sinners, and we dare to present offerings to God as if the Creator had a need for anything! Hence, it is normal for us to do it timidly, finding it surprising that the Almighty and All-Holy God deigns to be grateful for our poor gifts.

Since the Roman Canon asks throughout its consecratory prayer that God may be pleased with our sacrifice, the Prayer over the Gifts may seem to be an anticipation of the Consecration. But the Prayer over the Gifts does not give this impression when it is an introduction to the three other Eucharistic Prayers.

No doubt, certain Prayers over the Gifts seem to ask more than that God should be pleased with them, or rather they seem to envisage this more realistically. They seem to beg for the Consecration of the bread and the wine into the Body and the Blood of Christ, for graces which God will grant us in return for our gifts, and even for the fruits of Communion.

This is easily explained. However sublime the reality that is accomplished at the Consecration, it remains mysterious and invisible except to the eyes of faith. Our gifts, from one end of the Eucharistic Action to the other, do not change in

---

[12] For example, Gn 4, 4-5; 8, 21; Lv 1 to 7; Nm 28; 29; Pss 20, 4; 40, 7; 50, 8. 14; 51, 18-21; 66, 15-20; Sir 1-9; 50, 15; Wis 3, 6; Is 1, 13; 57 6; Jer 6, 20; 44, 21; Dn 3, 39-40; Hos 6, 6; 9, 4; Jl 2, 14; Mal 1, 6-14; 3, 4; 2 Mc 1, 26.

appearance. Even after the Consecration we continue to call them presents, offerings, bread, a cup. Similarly, already before the Consecration, we saw in them their ultimate destination. After all, the *matter* itself of the Sacrament was chosen by God so as to symbolize in advance its effects of vivification, comfort, union in peace and unity.

The final reason stems from a principle which holds good for the explanation of the whole Mass and especially the Eucharistic Prayer. Our minds tend to analyze, so as to discern the successive phases of a complex action as they discern the diverse parts of a living body. But just as the living body is *one,* so does the complex action possess a unity, and our analysis must not become a dissection. There are parts, there are turning points, there is progression in the Mass; but this does not mean that there is a succession of separate and independent acts.

If such a reflection is applicable to all the phases of the Mass, it is particularly valid for the Prayer over the Gifts which really plays the role of a hinge. By recapitulating the contribution of the gifts and giving them the meaning of an offering, it inevitably points to the Eucharistic Prayer to which it immediately introduces us.

V
THE EUCHARISTIC PRAYER

32. THE FOUR EUCHARISTIC PRAYERS

We must take the name "Eucharistic Prayer" in a precise
sense. It is not any prayer which has a relation to the Eucharist as, for example, a hymn of adoration sung before the
Blessed Sacrament. It is the central and most holy prayer of
the Eucharistic Liturgy. It is not merely a prayer: it *makes*
the Eucharist, but this efficacious Action is enveloped in a
prayer of thanksgiving which is very complex, a prayer of
offering, of petition, etc. It begins with the Preface and ends
with the Doxology: [1] "Through Him, with Him, in Him . . ."
which precedes the Our Father (the latter belongs to the rites
of Communion).

From its known origins and over the course of centuries
the Roman Liturgy has used only one Eucharistic Prayer
which for this reason has been called the *Canon.* [2] Since
1968, however, the Roman Liturgy has accepted three other
Eucharistic Prayers. Why, we might ask, was this multiplicity introduced?

---

[1] A doxology, from *doxa,* "glory," and *logos,* "word," is a formula
which celebrates the glory of God.

[2] This term comes from a Greek word which means, reed; hence suggests a rigid rule, a fixed formula.

It was inevitable that permission would be given to say the Canon aloud and in the living language of the people when there was only one Canon. It is not logical to use the living language for the parts that are relatively secondary in a liturgical function, yet keep the essential part of this function hidden under the veil of silence and a language foreign to most of the people.

To insist on retaining such secrecy could be interpreted as attributing some cabalistic or magic power to the materiality of words and not to their meaning. This in fact is contrary to one of the most fundamental axioms of Christian doctrine concerning the Sacraments, namely, that they are efficacious by reason of their signification.

But the use of the vernacular was bound to have a second result which had already been noticed when the "pericopes," or passages, drawn from Holy Scripture, and then the Orations and the Prefaces, were translated into the people's language. By removing the at times sumptuous and refined mantle of the Latin, we sometimes cruelly expose the poverty hidden under beautiful formulas.

Vernacular Highlights Defects of Texts

On the other hand, even admitting that certain texts still manifest in translation a great and substantial richness, the frequent repetition of these texts which have become directly intelligible begets a tiresome monotony. The Conciliar *Constitution on the Sacred Liturgy* had doctrinal reasons for envisaging a reorganization and profound enlargement of the Lectionary. However, a reading in the vernacular of pericopes repeated over and over at short intervals, in particular, those of the Common of the Saints, also showed that a Lectionary with more varied Readings was urgently needed.

Hence, in the United States, as in many other countries, an experimental Weekday Lectionary was approved and used. This acted as a kind of "trial-balloon" for the more complete and more satisfactory Lectionary mentioned above which will soon be used throughout the Church.

The same phenomenon was bound to take place regarding the Roman Canon. It has been shorn of the magnificent stylistic Latin in which it was clothed (or rather which contributed to its make-up, for the separation of the "fundamental substance" and the "form" is a scholastic idea that has no relation to the reality of the literary fact). It has also been translated as well as possible, eliminating pompous repetitions which would seem awkward or even ridiculous when expressed in modern language.

Nevertheless, it was seen to be full of repetitions and almost completely static in structure; this gives it the appearance of marking time and of being too drawn out. Hence, several attempts were made to improve and reorganize this text. But they all encountered difficulty, showing that the structure of the text was so solid as to be impossible of substantial modification without suffering disfigurement and even destruction.

It was then decided to respect this venerable monument of Roman culture and piety. Permission would simply be given to omit, at a later date, some conclusions which accentuate the impression of fragmentation, and to shorten some lists of Saints which were somewhat lengthy.

The Canon, therefore, could not undergo anything more than an external reform, that is, it was to be left almost the way the Roman tradition had passed it on to us. Other Eucharistic Prayers would be composed which, avoiding the defects we have briefly pointed out, would cast new light upon the Eucharistic Mystery, whose riches cannot be sufficiently emphasized by one sole formula.

New Eucharistic Prayers Added

Thus, the "Consilium" entrusted with the liturgical reform composed three "new" "anaphoras" [3] or Eucharistic Prayers. We place the word "new" within quotation marks because while the texts are new they are inspired by existing models.

The Second Eucharistic Prayer (counting the Roman Canon as the First) took as starting point the most ancient Latin anaphora known to us: the one given us by the Roman priest Hippolytus, less as a text used than as a schema, in his *Apostolic Tradition* dated at the beginning of the 3rd century.

The Third Eucharistic Prayer greatly resembles the Eastern Anaphoras. The Fourth follows closely the plan of the Second and the Third, but it multiplies Biblical allusions and considerably develops remembrances of the whole economy of salvation.

We have referred to Eastern Anaphoras. Henceforth the Latin Liturgy resembles the liturgies of the East by the simple fact that it can now make use of several different anaphoras, something which was always done by these liturgies, even if in reality they make use of only a small number. It is not our intention to give a commentary in turn of the four Eucharistic Prayers which may now be used in the Roman Rite. This has already been done very well by others. Besides, it would oblige us to take up once again, line after line, in a wearying fashion, texts which are already known to our readers through practice.

We believe that it is more interesting and useful to examine these four Eucharistic Prayers as a whole, paying more attention to what they have in common than to their differences. In this way we shall discover that they follow almost the same plan and set forth a common teaching.

---

[3] An "anaphora," from the Greek *ana-phero*, to bring up, to offer, means exactly the same thing as the Latin *oblatio*. What the Eastern Christians call "anaphora," we Westerners call "Eucharistic Prayer."

This method also offers a particular advantage in the event that other Eucharistic Prayers are published and authorized in the future. Whatever newness there might be in their expression, they could not depart very far from a plan which belongs to the nature of things, to a tradition that is as old as Christianity and even older, for it is linked up with the tradition of the Synagogue. [4]

Same Series of Fixed Points in All

If the plan of the new Eucharistic Prayers differs somewhat from what was formerly called the Roman Canon (and now "First Eucharistic Prayer"), it is also true that the same series of fixed points is found in all four. This remark may interest and comfort those who fear getting lost in that multiplicity of Eucharistic Prayers from among which the priest is free to make his choice.

All the Eucharistic Prayers begin with a dialogue of the priest with the faithful introducing the Preface, which ends with the *Sanctus* (Holy, holy, etc.).

All have as their center and their summit the words of the Institution pronounced by Christ at the Last Supper. The account in which they are framed can vary slightly, but the words of our Lord are always identical.

In all the Eucharistic Prayers, the account of the Institution is followed by an anamnesis [5] acclamation sung by the people, and the anamnesis prayer recited by the priest. Finally, all end and culminate in an identical doxology: "Through Him, with Him, in Him . . .," which the faithful conclude with a solemn *Amen.*

What follows after this, beginning with the Our Father, no longer belongs to the Eucharistic Prayer properly so-called,

---

[4] This has been shown most clearly by L. Bouyer in his *Eucharistie Théologie et spiritualité de la Prière eucharistique,* Desclée & Co., 1966.

[5] The word *anamnesis* means literally "commemoration" or "memorial"; we shall explain it fully in no. 35.

and does not vary, with the evident exception of the Communion Song and Psalm, and the Prayer after Communion which belong to the Proper of each Mass.

33. THE SONG OF THE ANGELS
AND OUR THANKSGIVING

Anyone who knows how to use a dictionary can find out that a "eucharistic" prayer is essentially eucharistic (thanksgiving), a prayer of thanksgiving. Today this Greek word *("eucharistia")* designates for us the Mystery of the consecrated bread and wine. It comes directly from the Gospel which says that Jesus took bread "after giving thanks." [6]

The entire Eucharistic Prayer unfolds in a thanksgiving, but the *keynote* is already given from the start, with the dialogue which precedes the Preface: "Lift up your hearts" (that is, let your thoughts rise to the most Divine plane)—"We lift them up to the Lord.—Let us give thanks to the Lord our God.—It is right to give Him thanks and praise."

This short dialogue is one of the most venerable elements of the Mass. It is found in all the liturgies and may go back to the Apostles. In view of its importance it is possible that it gave the name "Preface" (in the actual sense of a "prologue") to the Great Prayer which it introduces. This was the opinion of Tertullian.

But if it is the Great Prayer itself which directly received the name "Preface," then this cannot be understood as a preamble, like the prefaces found in modern books, words which do not form part of the text and hence are not always read. In this case, *praefatio* comes from *prae-fari* not in the sense of to "speak beforehand" but to "speak before (in front of)," to make a solemn proclamation "before the people."

---

[6] Or "after having blest": the two words are synonymous and mean praise addressed to God (cf. the references given above, p. 102, note 3).

In any case, it is essential, if we wish to understand the Eucharistic Prayer, to keep in mind that the Preface is not an introduction to the Prayer, but its solemn beginning or, as is said in music, its "overture" which presents some major *leitmotivs* of the opera. It is interesting to note in this respect that the Second and Fourth Eucharistic Prayers have a Preface incorporated into their text. [7]

The priest, after the people's assenting response, repeats his call for thanksgiving:

> Father, all-powerful and ever-living God,
> we do well always and everywhere to give You thanks
> through Jesus Christ our Lord.

"Thanksgiving" More than "Thank You"

But, once more, what is this "giving thanks"?

To render thanks is not, as one is too inclined to say immediately, the same as to thank someone. For a limited gift or service, we address a "thank you" to a benefactor; once we have thanked him, we are even with him. Of course, thanksgiving comprises gratitude, but in exchange for a total, all-embracing gift such as our being, our life; and toward an infinite Being, Who, therefore owes us nothing.

Hence, a sentiment which is dominant in "thanksgiving," but not in a mere "thank you," is the realization that we cannot render thanks (thanksgiving) sufficiently, because the benefit is a radical one—but let us note that, at the same time, the one who has been "graced" with such a gift, is not in the least lowered or humiliated by acknowledging it. He knows that it will never be possible to establish any proportion and of course any equality between him and an infinite Being.

---

[7] The Second Eucharistic Prayer (cf. above, no. 32), it is true has its own preface but it can be replaced by a proper Preface. The Fourth Eucharistic Prayer has a Preface that is obligatory and inseparable from it. As for the Roman Canon and the Third Eucharistic Prayer, no Preface is connected with either; one must be taken from those found in the general collection of Prefaces.

Besides, when he makes such an act of "thanksgiving" he does not respond to the Divine benefit by a mere human gratitude. It is the Divine grace he has received which He sends back up to God. The "thanksgiving" here is properly theologal: coming from God, addressed to God, and Divine in nature.

That is why it is inexhaustible, we repeat, in contrast with a simple "thank you" by which we have paid our debt for a finite gift. It is "gratitude" for an infinite debt which will never be paid. St. Paul recommends in season and out of season giving thanks in and for everything. We will render thanks for all eternity.

The Eucharistic Prayer is not a thanksgiving throughout, neither is the Mass. We must note, however, that the act of thanksgiving begins long before the Eucharistic Prayer, with the Entrance Song, the "Glory to God," the doxological conclusion of the Collect. But the Eucharistic Prayer receives from the Preface of thanksgiving its general tonality, which we characterize with two words calling it *lyrical* and *peaceful*.

The Eucharistic Prayer, in so far as it is an act of thanksgiving, is *lyrical*, because of the immensity and sublimity of its object. It is neither a reasoning discourse nor a simple profession of faith. As was said by St. Justin, in the oldest description of the Eucharist, the celebrant gives thanks "to the extent of his ability."

Hence, the entire Eucharistic Prayer, and not only the Preface, is enthusiastic, solemn, noble and poetic; and we now understand, what is no doubt a return to origins, why it is now permitted to the one celebrant, as well as to concelebrants, to sing this central part.

But since we know, without feeling anxiety or humiliation, that our thanksgiving will never equal the benefits received, our Eucharistic Prayer will be *peaceful*. Whether it be in the rendering of thanks, or in the Consecration, in the

anamnesis (memorial), or the invocation and the intercessions, which we shall consider later on, it will never be tense,
pathetic, or theatrical.

This is even more true since it is not the act of an individual, but of the liturgical assembly and of the whole Church.
Even when there is only one celebrant, he uses "we." And he
has, after all, asked the assembly to join him, by the preparatory dialogue. But, above all, the Preface ends by calling
upon the innumerable Blessed Spirits, whom we join in singing: "Holy, holy, holy, etc."

As we have said, thanksgiving is the eternal function of
the Blessed. It is in this sense that we may rightly speak of
the heavenly sacrifice. In heaven there will be no more sacrifice of reconciliation or expiation. Only its effects will remain. But the "sacrifice of praise" is eternal and already now
it unites the sacrifice of earth with the praise of the heavenly
Spirits and of all the Blessed.

Trinitarian Structure of Thanksgiving

The *structure* of the thanksgiving will in the end determine
the structure of the whole Eucharistic Prayer. It is a trinitarian structure, but not in the sense in which Western theology prefers to consider the unity of Nature in the Trinity
(this precisely is the perspective of the Preface of the Trinity [8]); rather it is trinitarian according to the Eastern perspective which is moreover the perspective of the whole liturgy.

The Divine Persons are considered according to their proper function in the Economy of Salvation. The Preface is addressed to the Father, as is insistently indicated by its first
words, and it passes "through" Christ. The latter is not the
One to Whom our worship is destined; He is its Mediator
and Priest.

---

[8] Formerly used on Sundays "of the year," the Preface of the Trinity
is now reserved for Trinity Sunday.

Finally, we must come back to the *object* of the thanksgiving. It comprises, as we have said briefly, the benefits we have received from God. The Jewish thanksgiving generally enumerates Creation and the Redemption, that is, the liberation from Egypt, the Pasch (cf. for example Ps. 136, the "Great Hallel").

In the Roman Canon, there is no question of Creation except in the prayer which immediately precedes the doxology: "Through Him, You give [create for] us all these gifts." The new Eucharistic Prayers speak of creation, right from the start; this is true especially of the Fourth Prayer.

But the Christian thanksgiving has as its principal object the Economy of Salvation and as its center, the Paschal Mystery. The succession of Roman Prefaces for the feasts of the annual cycle constitutes a very beautiful evocation of the Paschal Mystery. But this notification of the object of the thanksgiving belongs to an element which we shall analyze later on, namely, the anamnesis memorial.

Thanksgiving Is Sacramental Celebration

At the end of our study of the thanksgiving it is of capital importance to remember that the thanksgiving Action is neither a mere spiritual elevation nor a proclamation, since we have here a sacramental celebration, a prayer which is at the same time an Action. It is going to be *realized*, in the strongest sense of the term.

Our thanksgiving is Christ in person in His Sacrifice. Of ourselves we are incapable of worthily giving thanks for the Divine benefits God has bestowed upon us. But, as we have said already, we are neither anxious nor humiliated because of this insufficiency; for since our thanksgiving repeats and realizes the thanksgiving Action of Christ it will become concretized and incarnate in the Sacrifice of Christ: the thanksgiving flows into the Consecration.

34. "THIS IS MY BODY
WHICH WILL BE GIVEN
UP FOR YOU"

"And giving thanks to You He blessed the bread." "Again giving thanks to You, He blessed the cup." [9] The Gospel texts concerning the multiplication of the loaves and the institution of the Eucharist, and the Pauline passage concerning the Institution, use "giving thanks" and "blessed" indifferently. Thus, the two words seem synonymous, interchangeable.

The First and Third Eucharistic Prayers, on the contrary, have united the two words, thus making their meaning more precise. "Giving thanks," that is, accomplishing the rites of Thanksgiving, Jesus "blessed" the bread and the cup, that is, He brought about their Consecration. In the Biblical sense the word "bless," like "giving thanks," designates an elevation toward God.

In reality, even the blessings of the Ritual have for their ultimate purpose to make us use some object for the service of God and for His glory. And here, precisely, it is the bread and the wine which will, as it were, ascend Godward: this is the upward movement expressed by the Latin words for oblation, offering, as also by the Greek word for anaphora.

This then is the true and theocentric sense of the Consecration as realizing a sacrifice. The earthly elements, the bread and the wine, are divinized. They become the Body and the Blood of Christ, not only in their substantial reality, but

[9] The official English translation for these two phrases in the First and Third Eucharistic Prayers is slightly different (it already incorporates the meaning which the author will go on to draw from his literal translation) : "He took bread and gave You thanks and praise"; "Again He gave You thanks and praise, gave the cup, etc." The more literal translation used by the author has been retained in the text to enable the reader to follow his reasoning. [Tr.]

also in their sacrificial function: "This is My Body which will be given up for you,"[10] say *all* the Eucharistic Prayers.

"This is the cup of My Blood, the Blood of the new and everlasting Covenant. It will be shed for you and for all men so that sins may be forgiven." The sacrificial function of the Blood is still more explicit than that of the Body, the more so because it is the "Blood of the Covenant," and "shed . . . so that sins may be forgiven"; now, without a sacrifice there is neither covenant,[11] nor remission of sins (cf. Heb 9, 22).

Consecration Realizes the Covenant

Mention of the Covenant calls for another remark. The Consecration realizes the Covenant, that is, the union of men in one sole people, in one sole body, and the union with God of this people, this unified body. The sacramental Communion comes afterward to express, make explicit, and particularize this mystery of union for every communicant, but it is already realized in the sacrificial Consecration. This confirms the Catholic position, so clearly affirmed by St. Thomas to the effect that, in the Eucharistic Consecration, the whole Mass is realized.[12]

This global and essential character of the Consecration of the bread and the wine, shedding light on the whole ensemble of the Eucharistic Liturgy, is particularly manifested by the fact that our Lord, before consecrating the bread, broke it and "gave it to His disciples, and said: Take this, all of you, and eat it. . . ." Likewise, He "gave the cup to His

---

[10] *"Quod pro vobis tradetur"* (1 Cor 11, 24). The Greek text says only: "[which is] for you," and it has one variant: "[which is] broken for you." In Lk 22, 19: "[which is] given for you." In reality, these parts of a sentence lack a verb. If the verb is supplied, it can be put either in the present or in the future tense. The *Vulgate* Latin version uses the future for First Corinthians, and the present for Luke.

[11] Cf Gn 8, 20—9, 17; Ex 24, 1-8; Jos 8, 30-35; etc.

[12] *Summa Theol.*, III., Qu. 73, art. 1, resp. 3; Qu. 78, art. 1. Council of Trent, Session 13, Canon 4, Denz-Sch. 1654/886.

disciples, and said: Take this, all of you, and drink from it. . . ."

Yet we know that the breaking of the Bread, its distribution and that of the Cup will take place only later, as also the act of eating and drinking. But the Consecration, which does not change the appearance of the bread and wine, already prepares the Body and Blood of Christ to be taken in Communion, as a "true food" and a "true drink" (Jn 6, 55).

This mystery of unity is, therefore, fundamentally realized from the time of the Consecration.

How Is Consecration a Sacrifice?

How does the Consecration take place? We know it: by the words of Christ Himself, Whom the priest makes "present." [13] It is not the words of the priest that consecrate, but the words of Christ which are produced (we might say, broadcast) in a mysterious way; for in virtue of his ordination the priest received power from the bishop, thus becoming a depositary of the powers of Christ.

Since it is the almighty Christ Who says: "This is My Body," we believe that this is so, that here truly is His Body.

But how is this Consecration a "sacrifice"? We cannot answer this if we think a sacrifice is a death with the shedding of blood. This, of course, is the case with a historical, real, sacrifice like that of Christ's Death on the Cross, but it is not the case with a sacramental sacrifice, like the Eucharistic Sacrifice. Here neither body nor blood is seen, but our faith discovers them under the signs of bread and wine, from the time of the Consecration.

A whole theology has sought at any cost to find a bloody, painful, destroying, sacrifice in the Sacrifice which the Council of Trent, with common sense, has nevertheless declared

---

[13] Cf. above no. 6, p. 19, concerning the "presences of Christ."

to be "unbloody." This mistaken quest confuses two different levels, that of the historical sacrifice, and that of the sacramental sacrifice; these must remain distinct though they are at the same time closely bound together.

The same can be said about the oft repeated theory that there is a sacrifice in the Eucharist because the Body and the Blood of Christ, which were separated by His violent Death, are consecrated separately at the Last Supper and at the Mass. What makes this theory unconvincing is, first of all, the fact that the separation of the Body (or of the flesh) and of the Blood comes from the Western habit of considering flesh and blood as separate elements, whereas in Semitic language they together evoke one single reality.

Secondly, the Consecration does not act upon the Body and the Blood of Jesus; it affects only the twofold matter of bread and wine, to show that there is question of a complete repast. It is realized much less because the elements are separated than because they are added to each other. As for the twofold consecratory formula, it is explained by the fact that the formula of the consecration of the chalice, with the mention of the Blood of the Covenant, speaks more explicitly about sacrifice. [14] We must note, however, that the recent adoption of the Gospel expression "given up for you" has restored to the first Consecration its sacrificial significance.

Reasons Why Mass Is a Sacrifice

The Mass is a sacrifice first because it renews the Act of Jesus at the Last Supper, which was closely connected with the Passion. These two, the Supper and the Passion, constitute "the hour" of Jesus. All the Eucharistic Prayers bring

---

[14] Cf. St. Thomas. *Summa Theol.*, III, Qu. 73, art. 2, concerning the use of a twofold matter in the Eucharist. Concerning the more explicitly sacrificial signification of the Consecration of the wine, cf. Qu. 78, art. 3. See also our commentary in the annotated edition of *L'Eucharistie*, vol. I, pp. 420-422; vol. II, pp. 360-362.

this out at the beginning of their account of the Institution: "The day before He suffered . . ." (Euch. Pr. I); "Before He was given up to death . . ." (Euch. Pr. II); "On the night He was betrayed . . ." (Euch. Pr. III); "He always loved those who were His own in the world. When the *time* [hour] came for Him to be glorified by You, His heavenly Father, He showed the depth of His love" [15] (Euch. Pr. IV).

We should note this observation of the Second Eucharistic Prayer: "Before He was given up to death, *a death He freely accepted.*" Jesus had declared: "For this reason the Father loves Me because I lay down My life that I may take it up again. No one takes it from Me, but I lay it down of Myself. I have the power to lay it down, and I have the power to take it up again. Such is the command I have received from My Father" (Jn 10, 17-28).

In the case of animals, unconscious of being victims of the ancient sacrifice, the sacrifice was purely passive. In the case of a priest, the sacrifice is a free and meritorious act, even if it is accomplished through obedience, for it is a question of an obedience of love. The Sacrifice of Jesus is a perfect sacrifice, in which priest and victim are one same Person Who is perfectly free and perfectly willing. And it is also freely that Jesus has instituted His Sacrifice, commanding us to do what He had done.

Every Mass realizes a sacrifice, a voluntary act, free not only on the part of the priest who ritually accomplishes it, but on the part of Christ Who has instituted it and realizes it efficaciously by His own words, according to His own institution. [16]

---

[15] This evidently is reminiscent of Jn 13, 1. The evangelist is going to recount the story of the washing of the feet which for him is the symbolic equivalent of the Eucharistic Institution.

[16] In spite of pious considerations, like those of the Cure of Ars, concerning Christ's "obedience" to the words of the priest, such considerations reverse the roles: for when celebrating Mass the priest obeys the command of Jesus.

In order that there be sacrifice, it is not sufficient that there be a free gift of oneself, an acceptance of one's loss. It is also necessary that this gift, this "immolation," have a religious purpose, that it be offered to acknowledge the sovereign power of God. Such is truly the case in the Eucharist, since it is offered as an act of thanksgiving, that is, let us repeat, to recognize the total character of what we owe to God.

The Eucharist is also a sacrifice because it implies an essential relation to the Death and the Resurrection of our Lord, which have constituted His unique sacrifice. This relation will be manifested, immediately after the account of the Institution, by the anamnesis prayer, which, however, adds nothing to the Eucharistic Consecration. It was implied in it. But the anamnesis (memorial) will make explicit the relation which exists between the Eucharistic Sacrifice celebrated at this very moment and the unique Paschal Mystery of Jesus.

Every sacrifice, finally, aims at establishing us "in a Holy Communion" with God, says St. Augustine, whose definition of a sacrifice has become classical. The Consecration is therefore sacrificial also because it makes Communion possible. Once more, we must not look upon the Consecration as an isolated act, but as an act within the whole sacramental complex of the Mass, if we wish to see that it realizes a sacrifice.

35. "FATHER, WE CELEBRATE THE MEMORY OF CHRIST . . . WE OFFER . . ." (ANAMNESIS)

The anamnesis is called forth immediately by the conclusion of the words of Consecration: "You will do it in memory of Me." *Eis ten emen anamnesin:* the word anamnesis, like that of eucharist, is based upon the Greek of the Gospel and of St. Paul. [17]

Anamnesis means memorial or commemoration. But just as "thanksgiving" in our context means much more than a "thank you," so anamnesis is much more than a recollection or a souvenir. It is a concrete action, which exists outside subjective memory or remembrance. It is a pledge, a token, a testimony.

Although, in all the liturgies, the anamnesis is the proper object of the prayer which immediately follows the Consecration, the prayer is also much more than a prayer of commemoration. The anamnesis, like the action of thanksgiving, is an action, it consists in *doing* what Jesus has done, as He has commanded us: "Do this in memory of Me."

Mass Is a Memorial

And just as the whole Mass (and not only the Preface) is an act of thanksgiving, so is the whole Mass an anamnesis. St. Paul has said: "As often as you shall eat this Bread or drink the Cup, you proclaim the Death of the Lord, until He comes" (1 Cor 10, 26). In speaking thus, He does not enclose the anamnesis in Communion; he considers in its ensemble what he calls the "Supper of the Lord." And this proclaims not only His Death, but His Death "until He comes," that is, together with His Death all that follows and that prepares for His return, namely, the Resurrection and Ascension.

These are the three great events constituting the complete Paschal Mystery, which our Eucharistic Prayers offer as the content of the anamnesis. Other liturgies add the waiting for Christ, His return, etc.

---

[17] It was our intention to write this whole book in the most simple language. But it has seemed impossible to us to avoid using technical terms such as *anamnesis* and *epiclesis,* which can be replaced only by ponderous paraphrases. We shall say now immediately that if "anamnesis" means memorial, there is question here of a unique sort of memorial. Likewise, "epiclesis" means invocation, but a very special sort of invocation, as we shall see in the next chapter.

The new Eucharistic Prayers conform to the sober Roman tradition. The Second Eucharistic Prayer does not even mention the Ascension (for it was already contained in the Resurrection). The Fourth adds to the Death of Jesus "His descent among the dead" which is only a corollary of it; and it specifies: "His Ascension to Your right hand." Finally, two of them note that we make the anamnesis "ready to greet Him when He comes again" (Euch. Pr. III), "looking forward to His coming in glory" (Euch. Pr. IV). Hence, Christ's Return is within the perspective of the anamnesis, but it does not form part of it.

It is easy to understand why. An anamnesis (a commemoration, a memorial) cannot be concerned with anything but past events, or rather with accomplished facts. For we are not content with reawakening the souvenir of distant episodes, buried in the past. We posit a concrete Memorial: the Eucharist contains Christ in His Passion and His Death, in His Resurrection and His Ascension.

Since it is a sacrifice, it necessarily evokes His immolation through death. But the sacrifice is complete only if it attains its purpose, if it is pleasing to God, if He sanctions it.

The Resurrection constitutes this fruit and outcome of the Sacrifice of Christ which is accepted by the Father. The same is true of the Ascension which forms a unit with the Resurrection: it is in rising that Christ enters into His new life, in the glory of His Father. [18]

Since Christ is really present in the Eucharist as we believe, He is there as He is today, as risen, glorified, dwelling in heaven "at the right hand of the Father." But His Ascension is also the pledge of His return: "This Jesus, Who has

---

[18] We know from the reading of the Gospels that the Ascension is situated in direct line with the Resurrection. Sometimes it even seems to have taken place on the same day (cf. Mk 16, 14-19; Lk 24, 36-51; Jn 21, 1. 17). It is only in the Acts of the Apostles (1, 3) that St. Luke mentions forty days during which the risen Christ holds conversations with His disciples. The Ascension on the fortieth day marks the end of this intermediary period, but the glorification of Jesus began with the Resurrection.

been taken up from you into heaven, shall come in the same way as you have seen Him going up to heaven" (Acts 1, 11).

By the Eucharist we not only recall the dead and risen Christ; we hold Him, if we so dare to speak, under the appearances of bread and wine. As for His Coming, we do not commemorate it, since it is a future event; but, with the risen and glorified Christ, we possess the pledge of His Coming which sustains our hope. [19]

Anamnesis Acclamation

If we had wished to follow the succession of the rites in strict fashion, we should have spoken first of the anamnesis acclamation chanted by the faithful immediately after the Consecration. But in order to give an undestanding of the meaning of this acclamation it was necessary to give the explanations we have just given.

This acclamation is called for by Jesus' command (just uttered by the priest) to repeat what He did. This command is so striking that it elicits this acclamation, even before the priest has had a chance to pronounce his prayer of anamnesis. Furthermore, instead of being addressed to the Father, as is the whole Eucharistic Prayer uttered by the priest, it is addressed directly to Jesus, in accord with the spontaneous movement of popular devotion.

We are acquainted with the diverse formulas of this acclamation. [19a] They are all a paraphrase of the formula of St. Paul which we have already recalled: "As often as you shall eat this Bread and drink the Cup, you proclaim the Death of

---

[19] Cf. the antiphon of the Office of the Blessed Sacrament (Corpus Christi): "O Sacred Banquet, in which Christ is received, the memory of His Passion is recalled, the mind is filled with grace and a pledge of future glory is given to us."

[19a] In English there are four formulas (responding to the priest's invitation: Let us proclaim the Mystery of Faith): (a) Christ has died, / Christ is risen, / Christ will come again. (b) Dying You destroyed our death, / rising You restored our life. / Lord Jesus, come in glory. (c) When we eat this Bread and drink this Cup, / we proclaim Your Death, Lord Jesus, / until You come in glory. (d) Lord, by Your Cross and Resurrection / You have set us free. / You are the Savior of the world.

the Lord until He comes" (1 Cor 11, 26). These diverse forms of the acclamation simply develop this sentence somewhat by inserting therein the mention of the Resurrection, or "You restored life," between the memorial of His Death and the waiting for His return.

This acclamation, recently introduced in our liturgy, is a wonderful manifestation at the very heart of the Eucharistic Prayer of the active participation of the faithful in the Eucharistic Celebration of the Paschal Mystery, an expression of their baptismal priesthood.

The Mystery of Faith

We can now understand the meaning of the expression "Mystery of Faith" which the priest pronounces to call forth the acclamation of the faithful. There is no question here of recalling *one* of the Mysteries of Faith, not even that of the real presence. It is a question of recognizing that, in the Eucharist, *the* Mystery of Faith is realized, concretely recalled, and offered to our communion: it is the whole economy of salvation, the whole plan of God's love, for the salvation of the world, which is present before us, at this moment, and to which we are asked to unite ourselves.

Whole Mass Is an Anamnesis

But it is not sufficient to say, following St. Paul, that the "Supper of the Lord" is an anamnesis as a whole and globally. This desire to represent the plan of God can also be found in many of its parts.

The Entrance Song (if it suggests the theme of the feast), the Responsorial Psalm, and the Communion Song all evoke, in a lyrical way, the Paschal Mystery, though it is seen only from the particular point of view of the day. The Collect frequently recalls the Mystery celebrated as a motive for confidence in our petition.

But it is especially the Biblical Readings which have the role of recalling things. They are not historical, retrospective lessons, arousing our curiosity or reviving old souvenirs. We have repeated over and over, following the *Constitution on the Sacred Liturgy*, that Christ is present in them; He speaks to us and He challenges us through the inspired word. This word is addressed to faith, which adheres to the Word of God as to a living Mystery.

Finally, the Creed recalls the whole history of salvation: by involving our faith, we become actors of this history which is always in action. This goes to show, as is so powerfully expressed by Father Jungmann,[20] that the Liturgy of the Word is something quite different from an obligatory prelude, even an extrinsic one, to the Eucharistic Prayer. It flows directly from the very nature of the Mass, in as much as the latter is essentially a memorial, an anamnesis.

The anamnesis is also found in the Eucharistic Prayers, outside the anamnesis acclamation and prayer properly so-called. The Preface is a commemoration; it invites us to thanksgiving, and we have seen that by its nature the act of thanksgiving is total, global, all-embracing.

However our memory often fails and our weak power of giving full attention demand that light be projected strongly now on one then on another among the countless motives for thanksgiving. St. Gregory reduced the Prefaces of the Roman Missal to nine. And he even left us under the name of "Common Preface," a Preface that is absolutely devoid of motives; it is a simple schema which confines itself to rendering thanks through Jesus Christ without saying why.

The present reform has considerably enriched the repertory of our Prefaces which, when taken as a whole, form a perfect Creed, more detailed and more lyrical than the Symbol of the Apostles or that of Nicaea-Constantinople.

The Roman Canon also has some other elements of anamnesis: the second prayer after the Consecration: "accept them [these offerings] as once You accepted," which recalls the

---

[20] *La Grande prière Eucharistique,* Coll. *"L'Esprit liturgique"* (23), ch. 1.

sacrifices of Abel, Abraham and Melchizedek which long before the Pasch of Moses prefigured the Sacrifice of Christ. Finally, it includes with the proper *Communicantes* [21] the sober and profound memory of events that are at the origin of some great feasts: Christmas, Epiphany, Holy Thursday, Easter, Ascension, Pentecost. But outside these elements, which after all are considerable, the Roman Canon, in its movement, remains foreign to the Economy of Salvation.

It is on this point that the new Eucharistic Prayers differ profoundly from their older "sister" and, to my mind, surpass her. They are wholly within the Economy of Salvation. Hearing these prayers, we truly relive the whole of Sacred History; our faith is fostered and we receive an incomparable strength and comfort.

In this respect the richest of all is the Fourth. This explains why the account of the Institution comes much later in it than in the other Prayers; it first recalls the splendor of God in Himself, admired by the Angels, Creation, the first sin, the first covenants, the pedagogy of the Prophets, and finally the sending of the Son. In regard to the Incarnation, this Eucharistic Prayer is as detailed as the Creed, so much so, that to avoid repetitions, it would be preferable to use it in Masses which have no Creed. But at the same time this would be a pity, for the faithful who assist at Sunday Masses would thereby lose a magnificent fresco of Sacred History!

Anamnesis Prayer

We must now return to the anamnesis prayer properly so-called, to underline a capital point for the understanding of the Mystery of the Mass.

In our four Eucharistic Prayers, the anamnesis is designated in Latin by an adjective: *memores* (Euch. Pr. I, II, III)

[21] "In union with the whole Church we celebrate [observe the memory of] that day when Mary . . . gave this world its Savior; . . . when Jesus Christ, our Lord, was betrayed for us . . .; rose from the dead in His human body," etc.

or a participle: *memoriale celebrantes* (Euch. Pr. IV). In our English translations these words are translated by: "we celebrate the memory . . . recall . . . (Euch. Pr. I), "In memory of" (Euch. Pr. II), "calling to mind" (Euch. Pr. III), "we now celebrate this memorial of . . . we recall . . ." (Euch. Pr. IV). They terminate in what constitutes the axis of the Prayer: *Offerimus:* "We offer to You" (Euch. Pr. I), "We offer You" . . . (Euch. Pr. II, III, IV).

It is this *Offering* which is essential in the anamnesis, and the support of everything else. The "offering" was implicit in the Consecration. Looked at in a superficial way, the Consecration might seem to be a simple narrative. But with the eye of faith we discern a Consecration which realizes the presence of the Body and the Blood of Jesus under the appearances of bread and wine.

But there is more, and we could guess it by discovering that this Consecration produces a Sacrifice. For sacrifice is defined as an immolation within an offering. Jesus, at the Last Supper as well as on the Cross, offered Himself. [22] Since Christ tells us to do what He has done, we in our turn must *offer* Him.

At the Last Supper and on the Cross, He offered Himself, alone. But since the time when mankind was redeemed by the Cross and believers (through Baptism) have become His Body, at Mass it is always Jesus Who offers Himself to His Father, but inseparably from His Church, which cannot do what He did, in memory of Him, without offering Him.

To offer is a real, present Act. The anamnesis, based on this offering, is therefore truly a recalling—not a speculative and retrospective one, but one that is active, actual, and ef-

---

[22] "Walk in love, as Christ also loved us and delivered Himself up for us an Offering and a Sacrifice to God to ascend in fragrant odor" (Eph 5, 2). "It is now no longer I that live, but Christ lives in me. And the life that I now live in the flesh, I live in the faith of the Son of God, Who loved me and gave Himself up for me" (Gal 2, 20). "How much more will the Blood of Christ Who through the Holy Spirit offered Himself unblemished unto God. . . ." (Heb 9, 14); etc.

fective. All of us together celebrate the Mass when, with the whole Church, with Christ Himself, we offer to God His sacrifice in an action of thanksgiving and for the remission of sins, recalling His Paschal Mystery, always living and acting among us.

36. "LET YOUR SPIRIT . . . MAKE THEM HOLY"
(EPICLESIS)

Whatever be the active power of the Eucharistic Prayer, in realizing at the same time the thanksgiving, sacrificial Consecration, anamnesis, and offering of Christ, it remains a *prayer.* This means that the one who *pronounces* it does not consider himself as holding master words, words which he can use according to his fancy; [23] he must use them as a servant, a religious, a priestly officiant, who humbly obeys the command of Christ.

The priest is not content with giving thanks to the Father, obeying Christ, commemorating and offering the Sacrifice. He invokes God; He asks Him to help him, bless him, and accept his sacrifice.

The word *epiclesis* [24] merely means "invocation." But Eastern Christians have given it a technical and precise sense: namely, an invocation pronounced after the account of the Institution that the Holy Spirit may sanctify the offerings.

---

[23] The priest is not allowed to pronounce the consecratory words over bread and wine anywhere and in any way he might choose, outside the liturgical context, notably that of the Eucharistic Prayer, which when used by him shows he has the intention of doing what the Church does. This intention is one of the elements necessary for the validity of every Sacrament. Cf. Denz.-Sch. 1312/695 and 1611/854, *Summa Theol.,* Part III, Qu. 60, art. 8; Qu. 64, art. 8. The text of St. Thomas (Part III, Qu. 74, art. 2, Resp. 2) which is sometime quoted in a contrary sense, does not deal with this question for its own sake.

[24] Like *eucharist* and *anamnesis,* the word *epiclesis* comes from the Greek, but unlike them it is not found in the accounts of the Last Supper.

Subject of Controversy

This has been a subject of controversy. Latin Christians were scandalized because this would seem to say that Christ's words did not suffice to realize the Consecration. Was it not showing a lack of faith to ask, as if one were not sure of it, for something that had already been produced?

Eastern Christians on their part reproached the Latins for pretending to consecrate the Eucharist in a presumptuous way and without religious spirit. [25]

The objection of the Latins was based upon an idea of the Eucharist that excessively isolated the consecratory words. The Eucharistic Prayer forms a whole, and it is erroneous to seek to divide it into parts of which some are indispensable and others pure ornament, although it is normal to attribute to Christ's own words an efficacy far superior to that of the words with which the Church surrounds Christ's words of Institution. As Bossuet has excellently expressed it:

> ... To come back to the Mass, when we ask God to change the bread into His Body, or to accept the oblation we offer Him, or to have His Holy Angel present it at the heavenly altar, or to have pity on the living, or to have this oblation give relief to the dead, do we believe that God waits before doing these things for every moment when we shall speak to Him? Or course not! All this is the product of a human language which is unable to be explained except part by part. And God Who sees in our hearts at one glance what

---

[25] "Those who entrust the Consecration of the offerings to prayer, do not despise the words of the Savior, nor do they rely upon themselves, nor do they make the Mystery depend on something uncertain, namely, the prayer of man, as we reproach the Latins for doing" (Nicolas Cabasilas, *Explication de la Sainte Liturgie,* Sources Chrétiennes" 4, Ch. 29, p. 154). "That God, entreated by the supplicant, would hear this prayer and give the Holy Spirit to those who implore Him; that nothing is impossible to him who prays with faith: God Himself has affirmed this, and this is necessarily true. That such a result is assured to those who simply pronounce a particular word, this is not said anywhere" (*Ibid.,* p. 157).

we have said, what we are saying, and what we desire to
say, hears everything at suitable moments known to Him,
and He has no need to worry about the particular moment
or place in which He does so. . . . Now apply this doctrine
to the Prayer of the Greeks. There will then exist no more
difficulty. After the words of our Lord, they pray God to
change the gifts into His Body and into His Blood; this
may mean either the application of the thing to be done
or the more particular expression of a thing already done,
and we cannot conclude anything else from the precise
terms of the Liturgy. [26]

Epiclesis in the Roman Canon

If we were casting doubt on the certain efficaciousness of
Christ's words because we pray to obtain their effect, it would
be as much out of order to pray before the Consecration as
to do it afterward. St. Thomas has met this objection, concerning the *Quam oblationem* ("Bless and approve our offering, etc.," *before* the Consecration) which can be regarded
precisely as an "epiclesis" (though without an invocation of
the Holy Spirit) in which we ask that the Consecration may
be accomplished.

Objection. "It is, most certainly, the Divine power which
realizes *(operatur)* this Sacrament. Hence, it is superfluous
for the priest to ask for the achievement of this Sacrament
when he says: *Quam oblationem* . . . ('Bless and approve our
offering; make it acceptable to You, an offering in spirit and
in truth, the Body and Blood of Jesus Christ, Your only Son,
our Lord.')"

St. Thomas *answers*: "There is no contradiction *(non est
inconveniens)* when we ask from God something which we
are absolutely certain He will do. This is the way Christ (in
Jn 17, 1) asked for His glorification."

[26] Bossuet, *Explication de quelques difficultés sur la prière de la messe
à un nouveau catholique,* ch. 45-46).

When we take the term epiclesis in its broad sense, we may say that the Roman Canon has a second epiclesis, one placed after the Consecration, namely, the *Supplices*, for when we say: "we pray that Your angel may take this sacrifice to Your altar in heaven" what does this mean if not that we ask God to divinize it, to consecrate it? [27]

This offers less difficulty, for we pray that the Consecration may bear fruit for us. But is this really a secondary effect of the Consecration? Can we ever ask for the Consecration without asking that it be "accomplished" *for us*? Its purpose is not to make present the Body and the Blood of Christ in an absolute manner, that is, without relation to us.

To say this does not mean at all that we cast doubt on the reality of the Consecration, or cast aside transubstantiation for the benefit of some insufficient theory. Since it is precisely under the species of bread and wine that the Consecration makes Christ present, this Consecration surely has for its essential object to let *us* participate in the Sacrifice of Christ. Before saying: "This is My Body," "This is the Cup of My Blood," did not Jesus say: "Take and eat, all of you," "Take this, all of you, and drink from it"?

To conclude our examination of the Roman Canon, let us stress its almost tiresome obstinacy in asking God to bless and approve our offering, to make it acceptable to Himself. This had already been requested by the Prayer over the Gifts. Such insistence may be attributed to its judicial spirit, its desire to accomplish everything according to the rules.

But we must also recognize its profoundly religious spirit. In order for some of the Greeks to accuse the Latin priests of

---

[27] "The altar in heaven [or on high]" means either the triumphant Church herself in which we ask to be admitted; or God Himself in whose life we ask to participate. Cf. *Summa Theol.*, Part III, Qu. 83, art 41, Resp. 9. Father de la Taille has given numerous liturgical and patristic testimonies to the effect that the "altar in heaven" is Christ, but the glorified Christ, and that the transfer of the offerings to this altar means nothing else than the Eucharistic Consecration (*Mysterium Fidei, elucid. XXI*).

consecrating the Eucharist in an off-hand manner, they had to isolate the consecratory prayers from the whole context of humble petitions in which they are enshrined.

The only reproach that could be made against the Roman Canon is that it never mentions the Holy Spirit at any moment in all these invocations, which cannot therefore qualify as an epiclesis in the proper sense of the term. It is well known that, during the Council, representatives of the East repeatedly expressed their regret because of the insignificant place given to the Holy Spirit in the theology and the Liturgy of the Latins.

Epiclesis in New Eucharistic Prayers

The new Eucharistic Prayers have, on their part, made up for this lacuna. Every one of these three Prayers has two epicleses, situated before and after the Consecration, and in both of them there is a petition to God for the gift of the Holy Spirit. For we must note that the epiclesis is never an invocation addressed to the Holy Spirit. It is an invocation directed to the Father to obtain His Spirit.

The Liturgy, except for some texts of Pentecost, never addresses the Spirit. No Prayer is ever directed to Him and no Feast is consecrated to Him. Pentecost is not a Feast of the Holy Spirit but, like all the Feasts of the liturgical year, it is a Feast of Christ: at Pentecost, He accomplishes His promise, He manifests His glory, and He founds His Church by the gifts of His Spirit.

The first epiclesis asks for the Consecration: "Let Your Spirit come upon these gifts to make them holy, so that they may become for us the Body and Blood of our Lord Jesus Christ" (Euch. Pr. II). "We ask You to make them holy by the power of Your Spirit, that they may become the Body and Blood of Your Son, our Lord Jesus Christ" (Euch. Pr. III). "Father, may this Holy Spirit sanctify these offerings.

REASON FOR THE EPICLESIS

Let them become the Body and Blood of Jesus Christ our Lord" (Euch. Pr. IV).

The last two formulas we have quoted simply ask for the Consecration. The first, like that of the Roman Canon (Euch. Pr. I), asks it "for us." We have already noted that the Consecration is necessarily "for us," since it acts upon bread and wine which will be given to us. Hence, it would be wrong to say that the "for us" takes something away from the objective reality of the Consecration requested.

Those four epicleses, including *"Quam oblationem"* ("Bless and approve our offering: make it acceptable to you," etc.,) of the Roman Canon, are accompanied by the imposition of hands, a traditional sign of the gifts of the Spirit in all the Sacraments: Baptism, Confirmation, Penance, Ordination. [28]

In the four Eucharistic Prayers, this epiclesis with the imposition of hands immediately precedes the account of the Institution. This shows most clearly that the latter is not a simple narrative, merely something called back to memory, but that it is an efficacious Consecratory Action.

Reason for the Epiclesis

Why do we ask especially for the gift of the Holy Spirit? Because the Eucharistic Consecration is a prolongation and a consequence of the Incarnation which was accomplished by the action of the Holy Spirit (cf. Mt 1, 18-20; "she was found to be with child by the Holy Spirit . . . that which is begotten in her is of the Holy Spirit"; and Lk 1, 35: "The

---

[28] The Apostles "after they had prayed," laid their hands upon those who were to be their collaborators and who, no doubt, were the first deacons (Acts 6, 6). Paul and Barnabas received the imposition of hands before they departed for their mission (Acts 13, 3). St. Paul writes in his Second Letter to Timothy (2, 6-7): "I admonish you to stir up the grace of God which is in you by the laying on of my hands. For God has not given us the spirit of fear, but of power and of love and of prudence."

Holy Spirit shall come upon you and the power of the Most High shall overshadow you."

Moreover the Consecration is a sanctification. These two words, in Biblical language, are synonymous. That is why we can translate in Christ's Priestly prayer (Jn 17, 17. 19) either: "Consecrate them in truth. . . . For them I consecrate Myself," or: "Sanctify them in the truth. . . . For them I sanctify Myself."

Hence the Consecration, or Sanctification, is the work which is proper to that Person of the Holy Trinity Who bears par excellence the title of *Holy.* All three Divine Persons are equally holy, of course, but it is the proper role of the Third Person, Who is also called Gift and Love, to impart holiness. In Eucharistic Prayers II and III, this idea of sanctification is quite naturally connected with the chant of *Holy, holy, holy!*

Finally, it is the proper work of the Holy Spirit to complete the work of the Father and of the Son; for this reason He is called the "Finger of the Father's Right Hand." [29] The Fourth Eucharistic Prayer says so explicitly in introducing the epiclesis: "He gave Himself up to death; but by rising from the dead, He destroyed death and restored life. And that we might live no longer for ourselves but for Him" (which is an excelent definition of holiness) "He sent the Holy Spirit from You, Father, as His first gift to those who believe, to *complete* His work on earth and *bring* us the fullness of grace."

That is why the Creed, after recalling Creation, the work of the Father, and Redemption, the work of the Son, attributes to the Holy Spirit the Church and the Communion of Saints *(communio sanctorum)* which can also be translated as the "communication of holy things *(sancta),*" which,

---

[29] In the "Come, Creator Spirit." This image comes from bringing together Matthew 12, 28: "If I cast out devils by the Spirit of God . . ." and Luke 11, 20: "If I cast out devils by the finger of God . . ."

evidently comprise the Sacraments and principally the Eucharist. [30]

The "Second" Epiclesis

The second epiclesis comes *after* the Consecration. Its purpose is to ask that the Consecration be accomplished. This shows not that we doubt the efficacy of the words of Consecration, but that these words do not form an independent "block," with the rest of the Eucharistic Prayer acting only as a frame, or an accessory ornament. We must not dismember or dissect the Eucharistic Prayer; this truth we can never sufficiently repeat.

Why do we make Christ present? Not merely to assure His presence among us, for it is already realized by all kinds of other means, [31] but to make His substantial and personal presence under the forms of bread and wine, which we can eat and drink, the means of our union with Him, in His Sacrifice, and also with our brethren. This is a work that is especially attributed to the Holy Spirit, Who is the Union between Father and Son, the Spirit of Giving and Gift, [32] of Communion and Love, unifying and vivifying "soul" of the Church.

Let us now see what the Eucharistic Prayers say about this activity of the Holy Spirit. "May all of us who share in the Body and Blood of Christ be brought together in unity

---

[30] The *Constitution on the Sacred Liturgy* notes that "From that time onward [after Pentecost] the Church has never failed to come together to celebrate the Paschal Mystery: ... celebrating the Eucharist, ... giving thanks ... in Christ Jesus 'in praise of His glory' (Eph 1, 12) through the power of the Holy Spirit" (art. 6) (*italics added*).

[31] We must therefore reject the sentimental considerations which envisage Jesus instituting the Eucharist because He did not have the heart to leave us! Not one Gospel text authorizes such an interpretation. On the contrary: "I speak the truth to you; it is expedient for you that I depart" (Jn 16, 7), "If you loved Me, you would indeed rejoice that I am going to the Father" (Jn 14, 28).

[32] The "Goodwill of Father and Son" (Father Whitford, 1530). [Tr.]

by the Holy Spirit" (Euch. Pr. II). "Grant that we, who are nourished by His Body and Blood, may be filled with His Holy Spirit, and become one body, one spirit in Christ" (Euch. Pr. III). "Lord, . . . by Your Holy Spirit, gather all who share this Bread and Wine, into the one body of Christ, a living sacrifice of praise" (Euch. Pr. IV).

All these epiclesis prayers, including the *Supplices* (Almighty God, we pray . . . let us be filled with every grace and blessing": Euch. Pr. I), come exactly at the right place, that is, immediately after the anamnesis prayer. There then we have the prayer which asks for the most holy object, for the very end and purpose of the Eucharist, beyond the presence of Christ and of His Mysteries, beyond His Sacrifice: we ask for the very fruit of the Sacrifice, which is: the profound unity of the Mystical Body.

The Fruit of the Eucharist

In two of our new Eucharistic Prayers, the fruit of the Eucharist is expressed in a way that is even more sublime, more demanding, more mysterious. In the Third Prayer, it forms the beginning of a new petition: "May He make us an everlasting gift to You," more clearly expressed: "May He, the Holy Spirit, as we become filled with Him, make us an eternal offering to His glory. . . ." In the Fourth Prayer, the same thing is asked and forms the conclusion of the epiclesis itself: "By Your Holy Spirit, gather all who share this Bread and Wine, into the one body of Christ, a living sacrifice of praise," which means, more explicitly expressed: "Grant to all who will share this Bread and drink this Cup to be reassembled by the Holy Spirit in one single body, *in order that they themselves be, in Christ, a living sacrifice to the praise of Your glory.*" [33]

---

[33] "To the praise of His glory" comes from Ephesians 1, 12 and 14.

This beautiful petition had been used in the Roman Missal for a long time in the Prayer over the Gifts on the Monday of Pentecost, which was used again on Trinity Sunday [34] (the Prayer over the Gifts often contains an anticipated epiclesis). This constitutes the last fruit of every Mass. The Conciliar *Constitution on the Sacred Liturgy* had enunciated this doctrine by recommending the participation of the faithful in the Mass:

> By offering the Immaculate Victim, not only through the hands of the priest, but also with him, they should learn to offer themselves too. Through Christ the Mediator, they should be drawn day by day into ever closer union with God, and with each other, so that finally God may be all in all [35] (art. 48).

This then is the ultimate fruit of participation in the Liturgy. But it transcends, goes beyond, the Liturgy. This was pointed out by the Conciliar *Constitution* in the passage where it shows the limits of the Liturgy which "does not exhaust the whole activity of the Church" (art. 9).

For this involves evangelization with a view to Baptism, which provides the Liturgy with its subjects, the persons who will participate in it. But besides this, the Liturgy itself calls for personal holiness, beyond that of official and community worship:

> The spiritual life, however, is not limited solely to participation in the Liturgy. The Christian is indeed called to pray with his brethren, but he must also enter into his chamber to pray to the Father, in secret (cf. Mt 6, 6); yet more, according to the teaching of the Apostle, he should

---

[34] "O Lord, we beseech You, sanctify these gifts, and having received the offering of this spiritual victim, *let us become an everlasting gift that is worthy of You.*"

[35] This recalls the words of St. Augustine: "This is the sacrifice of Christians that we, who are many, may form one single body, in Christ. It is this the Church accomplishes in the sacrament of the altar, well known by the faithful, where it is manifest that she is offered in that which she herself offers" (*City of God*, Bk 10, ch. VI).

pray without ceasing (cf. 1 Thes 5, 17). We learn from the
same Apostle that we must always bear about in our body
the dying of Jesus, so that the life also of Jesus may be
made manifest in our bodily frame (cf. 2 Cor 4, 10. 11).
This is why we ask the Lord in the sacrifice of the Mass
that, "receiving the offering of the spiritual victim," He
may fashion us for Himself "as an eternal gift" [36] (art. 12).

Moreover, St. Paul demands: "I exhort you therefore,
brethren, by the mercy of God, to present your bodies as a
sacrifice, living, holy, pleasing to God—your *spiritual service* [that is,your *spiritual worship*]" (Rom 12, 1). Liturgical
worship consists in *offering* Christ; the spiritual worship, of
which it is the expression and the source, consists in *offering ourselves* with Him. It is *"spiritual"* worship because it
is animated by that Spirit Whose intervention we have
asked for in the epiclesis.

37. PETITIONS FOR THE CHURCH AND FOR ALL MEN

The epiclesis prayers end with the perspective of the
heavenly glory, for we ask to be transformed into "an eternal offering of praise of Your glory," and this is accomplished only in heaven. The end of the Eucharistic Prayer
thus resumes its initial theme, where the Preface affirmed
that our action of thanksgiving unites us to the Angels, and
to "(all) the Saints" (Euch. Pr. II) in order that we may sing
(with one voice): "Holy, holy, holy!"

We see, therefore, that the Saints have a place in the Eucharistic Prayer, by what we sometimes call "intercessions"
and through which we present a certain number of petitions to God. These intercessions raise two kinds of difficulties.

---

[36] Prayer over the Gifts of Pentecost Monday, cited in note 34.

First Difficulty of Intercessions

First difficulty. Is it not shocking to see a part of a "Eucharistic Prayer," which is therefore God-centered, turn away from God?

Response: To declare that a prayer of petition is foreign to a prayer of thanksgiving is to have an overly geometric concept of prayer. In every living prayer these two intermingle. [37]

The act of thanksgiving prepares for and introduces the petition, for it shows God that He is not in the presence of ungrateful persons. And the petition shows the confidence that the action of thanksgiving has produced in us. This is true in that school of prayer we call the Psalter. All the so-called "thanksgiving" Psalms have an important section for supplication. [38]

On the other hand, this supplication is not self-centered and egoistic; there one prays much for one another, one prays before all for the Church, and this is the very end-purpose of the whole Eucharist.

Second Difficulty of Intercessions

Second difficulty. The Eucharistic Prayer portrays Christ as Priest and Mediator; is it right then to have also recourse to the intercession of mere creatures such as the Saints? An allied difficulty is the one raised by the celebration of Mass in honor of the Saints, either because the Liturgy prescribes it or permits it on their feast day, or because the faithful ask the priest to say Mass "in honor" of some particular Saint.

---

[37] Cf. 2 Cor 9, 14; Phil 4, 6; Col 4, 2 and especially 1 Tm 2, 1, a classical text which St. Thomas comments on in *Summa Theol.*, Part II of the Second, Qu. 83, art. 17.

[38] Cf. especially Psalms 22, 31, 35, 40, 115-116 (cf. also P. Drijvers, *Les Psaumes, genres littéraires et thèmes doctrinaux*).

Bossuet gives a vigorous response to this allied objection: "In reality the one who makes such an objection must have an overly materialistic bent and one that is closed to heavenly things, for he does not see that paying honor to Saints is not so much honoring them as honoring God." And after mentioning numerous examples of this fact taken from the various liturgies, he concludes: "You see what is the meaning of offering for the Saints: it means celebrating the greatness and the power of God in the graces they have from Him." [39]

In regard to the intercession of the Saints, when we look at it carefully, we find that it is invoked with the utmost discretion. In the Roman Canon, where the Saints have a particularly important place, this invocation is found only in one prayer, namely, in the *Communicantes:* "In union with the whole Church we honor Mary . . . Joseph, the Apostles. . . . May their merits and prayers gain us your constant help and protection. Through Christ our Lord" (Euch. Pr. I, before the Consecration).

When we examine the three new Eucharistic Prayers, we find that the intercession of the Saints is invoked only in the Third which reads: "May He [the Holy Spirit] make us an everlasting gift to You and enable us to share in the inheritance of Your Saints, with Mary, the virgin Mother of God; with the Apostles, the Martyrs, Saint N. . . . and all Your Saints, *on whose constant intercession* we rely for help."

In all these prayers in which the Saints are named, what we ask before all else is that we may join them and share their blessedness. Even when their intercession is invoked, in the only two cases mentioned, it is only as a secondary consideration.

[39] Bossuet, *op. cit.*, ch. 40.

Moreover, it is normal to invoke the Saints in the course of the Eucharist. They are not strangers, since the Eucharist gives us "a pledge of future glory" (Antiphon, Second Vespers of Corpus Christi), which they already possess. Does the Eucharist not aim at transferring the whole Church of earth to heaven?

Notable Difference in New Prayers

With respect to the petitions we are presently examining, the new Eucharistic Prayers present still another notable difference from the Roman Canon. In the latter, these prayers are almost equally distributed before and after the Consecration. In both places there are two long lists of Saints (which the priest is now permitted to shorten). This arrangement which is wholly proper to the Roman Canon, does not seem to have any doctrinal motif behind it. No doubt it is to be attributed to a desire for symmetry. This is in line with the somewhat static and truncated character of the Roman Canon which likes parallels and repetitions.

This could not be the way of the new Eucharistic Prayers which follow the sweep of Salvation History. Just as, in the Creed, the mention of the Church and her Sacraments comes as a finale, under the insignia of the Holy Spirit, so do the prayers for the Church in the new Eucharistic Prayers come "at the end of time," that is, after recalling Creation, the Incarnation, the Redemption, and the Institution of the Eucharist.

This is a very natural and quasi-necessary order. At the same time, as we have already remarked, this order realizes a sort of inclusion; with the Preface, the Eucharistic Prayer began with the evocation of the citizens of heaven who participate in our song of thanksgiving, and it ends with the invocation of the Saints whom we hope to join in that glory which will be celebrated by the concluding doxology: "Through Him, with Him, in Him . . ."

Prayer for All Men

There were some who reproached the Roman Canon for being exclusively "ecclesiastical" in its petitions, in the sense that its horizon seems to go no farther than the actual members of the Church. This is not so, for the Eucharist makes present the Sacrifice of the Cross which Jesus has offered for all men.

Again, the Church is not a closed society. It is potentially the whole of mankind, because "God our Savior wants all men to be saved" (1 Tm 2, 4). When we ask God to gather His Church in unity, to *"coadunare"* the Church, it means more than to assemble it in *its* unity: it means to increase the one Church, to make all mankind enter it.

The new Eucharistic Prayers bring to light this missionary aspect, this concern for those who are far away. Thus: "Remember our brothers and sisters who have gone to their rest in the hope of rising again; bring them and *all the departed* into the light of Your presence" (Euch. Pr. II). "Welcome into Your kingdom . . . *all who have left this world* in Your friendship. . . . In mercy and love unite *all Your children wherever they may be*" [40] "Lord, remember those for whom we offer this sacrifice, . . . those here present and all Your people, and all who seek You with a sincere heart. Remember also those who have died in the peace of Christ and all the dead whose faith is known to you alone" (Euch. Pr. IV).

38. GLORY TO THE FATHER, THROUGH THE SON, IN THE SPIRIT (DOXOLOGY)

The last sentences of the Four Eucharistic Prayers could be signed by St. Paul. All the petitions in which they conclude are centered on Jesus and recapitulated in Him. The

---

[40] The French translation reads: "all Your children who are dispersed" (Euch. Pr. III). [Tr.]

formula of the Roman Canon remains one of the most beautiful expressions of this recapitulation. [41] "Through Him You give us all these gifts, You fill them with life and goodness, You bless them and make them holy." [42]

In the Second Eucharistic Prayer, which is very short, this connection with the final doxology is reduced to its most simple expression: "May we praise You in union with them [all the Saints] and give You glory through Your Son, Jesus Christ." The Third and Fourth recall the Roman Canon: "From Whom all good things come" (Euch. Pr. III); "Through Whom You give us everything that is good" (Euch. Pr. IV).

But these words are less a conclusion than a transition to what will be the solemn conclusion of the Eucharistic Prayer, namely, the Doxology. Here again we must refer to St. Paul whose letters are punctuated with this type of brief hymn to the glory of God. [43]

But, at Mass, the priest is not satisfied with pronouncing words of praise. He makes a gesture. He raises with one hand the paten that holds the consecrated Hosts, and with the other the chalice filled with the precious Blood (or if

---

[41] "To recapitulate" exactly translates the Greek of St. Paul (Eph 1, 10): *anakephalaiousthai,* to gather and renew all by bringing it under one sole Head (*kephale*: head).

[42] The French translation seems to put things more clearly: "It is by Him that You do not cease to create all those goods, that You bless them, You give them life, You sanctify them and make a gift of them to us." [Tr.]

[43] It may be useful to recall a few: "For from Him and through Him and unto Him are all things. To Him be the glory forever, amen" (Rom 11, 36). "To the only wise God, through Jesus Christ, be honor forever and ever. Amen" (Rom 16, 26, end of the Epistle). "Grace and peace be to you from God the Father, and from our Lord Jesus Christ, Who gave Himself for our sins, that He might deliver us from the wickedness of this present world, according to the will of our God and Father: *to Whom is glory forever and ever. Amen*" (Gal 1, 3-5). "To the King of the ages, Who is immortal, invisible, the one only God, be honor and glory forever and ever. Amen" (1 Tm 1, 17) (*italics added*). There are also beautiful doxologies in the Book of Revelation.

there is a deacon, it is he who raises the chalice), and he solemnly sings the formula of praise which gives the meaning of his gesture, while the gesture gives to the formula an extraordinary importance.

Meaning of Doxologies

The doxologies often seem ambiguous, because it is not clear whether they wish to affirm, recognize, and proclaim the glory of God, or to long for and adhere to it. We met with a similar ambiguity in the *Dominus vobiscum:* "The Lord be (or is?) with you." Here, however, there is no ambiguity, for it is quite certain that we are in the presence of an affirmation.

This is all the more important since in our modern language we understand by glory a sort of reflection of greatness which depends on fame. But this is not the Biblical sense of the word glory *(kabod)* which evokes the *weight* and fullness of the Divine Being, although the Greek word chosen to translate the Hebrew word *kabod* is *doxa* which means first of all opinion, hence glorious renown.

In contrast with the *Dominus vobiscum,* the Latin phrase here has a verb, a verb in the indicative and not in the subjunctive: *est* (is). Our English translation of the great doxology which terminates the four Eucharistic Prayers is explicit: "All glory and honor *is* Yours, almighty Father, for ever and ever. Amen." In other words, it is not a question of wishing or procuring His glory for God, but of recognizing it: we have a certainty and a guarantee of this in the Consecrated Gifts which the priest has in his hands and raises in a gesture intended both to show and to offer.

The possessor of this glory and the One for Whom this praise is intended is God, the Father almighty, as He was also the One to Whom the thanksgiving of the Preface was addressed.

As in the Preface, the Son is the Mediator, *"through Him."* But if the Mediator is first distinct from the two extremes which He alone can bring together, when His work of mediation is accomplished, these two extremes are united to Him and are united in Him. Now that the Sacrifice of the Covenant is accomplished, we have joined our Mediator; it is *with Him* and *in Him* that we glorify the Father.

"In the unity of the Holy Spirit." This is a faithful "offset" of the Latin *in unitate Spiritus Sancti.* But this does not make it any less obscure. It is not a question of an abstract and static "unity," which would be the proper attribute of the Holy Spirit; it is a question of the action He exercises, an action of union, of communication, of communion: *koinonia,* in Greek. It is a recollection of the epiclesis: through the Holy Spirit, or rather in Him, we have become one single offering to the eternal praise of the Father.

To this solemn proclamation of the glory of the Father, through the Son, in the Spirit, the people answer with a solemn: *Amen.* But, note, here it does not mean "So be it"— for we are in the presence of an affirmation—but "It *is* true!" "We *are* certain of it!" "We applaud!"

VI
COMMUNION RITE

39. THE OUR FATHER AND ITS CONCLUSION

With the Doxology the Eucharistic Prayer has come to an end; the essence of the Sacrifice has been achieved. The immolated Christ has been offered to the Father and we with Him. The only thing that now remains is for us to express our participation in His Sacrifice by the administration—what a horrible word which we should do better to translate by: the serving—of Communion. All the rites that now follow have as their object to prepare for and then realize Communion.

The Our Father has always been considered a preparation for Communion because of two of its petitions. First, its petition for bread. This brings up an almost insoluble problem because in Matthew, whose Our Father is the only one which has become liturgical, the bread is qualified as *epiousion*, a rare and obscure Greek term.

Our "Daily" Bread

We are not permitted to translate it by "daily" because this term comes from Luke, where we ask "give us every day *(quotidie)* the *epiousion* bread," which is not in line with the filial and totally trustful dispositions toward Providence recommended by Jesus (cf. Mt 6, 25-34; Lk 12, 22-31). [1] In St. Matthew we ask "Give us today our *epiousion* bread."

---

[1] "Do not be anxious for your life, what you shall eat. . . . Look at the birds of the air. . . . Your heavenly Father feeds them . . ." (Mt 6, 25-34) ; "Do not seek what you shall eat. . . . Your Father knows you need these things" (Lk 12, 22-31).

We can translate this word by "of tomorrow," "of the future." The official Latin translation, called the Vulgate has translated it by "super-substantial," that is, supernatural. But this translation in spite of its evident Eucharistic meaning, has not been adopted by the Roman Missal which unfortunately has preferred the term *quotidianum* ("daily").

The "ecumenical" French translation of this text of the Our Father reads: "Give us today our bread of that day." But this is not a pure repetition, if we understand "that day" as the Day of the Coming of the Lord, in connection with the preceding petition: "Your kingdom come." So this French translation which seems naive or even silly would then combine the translations which speak of a bread to come and those which speak of a supernatural bread.

On the other hand, the English ecumenical text [1a] has chosen to use the following translation: "Give us today our *daily* bread." The reason given for this decision is: "In fact, the petition is for the food of the heavenly banquet, and the familiar 'daily bread,' from which there is no reason to depart on grounds of accuracy, is in harmony with the eschatological interpretation and the tradition, liturgical and patristic, which refers the phrase to the Eucharist."

"Forgive Us Our Trespasses"

Another petition of the Our Father prepares for Communion. It is the one in which we beg God to pardon our offenses, as we pardon those who have offended us. Here also there is a contamination of the Our Father of Matthew

---

[1a] This text, however, has *not* been approved for liturgical use although the ecumenical texts for other parts of the Mass have been introduced into the official English translation. [Tr.]

by the Our Father of Luke. In Matthew our Lord says: "Forgive us our debts, as we also forgive our debtors" (Mt 6, 12). This image of the debt, as well as the obligation of forgiving our debtors, in view of our own much more considerable debts toward God, is then developed in the parable recorded by Matthew (18, 21-35), in which a man who owes a king a debt of millions of dollars is pardoned and then goes and refuses to forgive a paltry debt to one of his own debtors.

The image of "debts" to signify sins was common among the Jews. Luke, who addressed himself to pagans, substituted the proper word for this image, without changing the esentials of the comparison, which then limps: "forgive us our sins, for we also forgive everyone who is indebted to us" (Lk 11, 3).

The French have adopted this translation because the Protestants still use it. But it is not satisfactory, for there is no common measure between the "offenses" that may be inflicted on us, simple creatures, and the offenses we are guilty of with respect to an infinitely holy God. On the contrary, the image of "debts," precisely because it is an image and not a definite concept, fits both cases though they are disproportionate. The Eastern Christians say: "Forgive us our debts as we forgive our debtors."

(The English ecumenical text has chosen to use: "Forgive us our sins as we forgive those who sin against us," thus falling into the very trap warned against by the above remarks. In this respect, the text retained for the Liturgy is superior to it: "Forgive us our *trespasses* as we forgive those who *trespass* against us." [Tr.]

Immediately after the end of the Our Father, Jesus, in St. Matthew (6, 14-15), says the following: "For if you forgive men their offenses, your heavenly Father will also forgive you your offenses. But if you do not forgive men, neither will your Father forgive you your offenses."

It is easy to make an application to Communion. We must approach it with a heart that is pure, innocent of every voluntary sin. But God cannot forgive us unless we ourselves are without a voluntary resentment against our neighbor. This application is already found a little earlier in the Sermon on the Mount: "Therefore, if you are offering your gift at the altar, and there remember that your brother has anything against you, leave your gift before the altar and go first to be reconciled to your brother, and then come and offer your gift" (Mt 5, 23-24).

This text invites us to pardon our neighbor before we make the offering. That is why in olden times the kiss of peace which expresses this reconciliation, took place at the moment of the presentation of the gifts. But, since we admit that the Eucharistic Liturgy forms a whole, we see no inconvenience in making this gesture of the "kiss of peace" at the moment of Communion, for Communion better expresses fraternal charity, by the procession and especially by the partaking of One same Bread. The presentation of the gifts no longer has the same value of an offering as it had at a time when everyone could bring his own household bread.

"Lead Us Not into Temptation"

The Our Father ends with one last request: [2] "Do not bring us to the test, but deliver us from evil," or "from the Evil one." Some are scandalized at the thought that God might submit us to the "test," temptation, and they quote a text from the Epistle of St. James: "Let no man say when he is tempted, that he is tempted by God; for God is no tempter to evil, and He Himself tempts no one" (Jas 1, 13). But the Greek text of the Our Father and the Latin transla-

---

[2] Certain Fathers of the Church found seven petitions in the Our Father, no doubt because of the symbolic value of the number seven. It seems to us that there are only six. In any case the last two sentences are closely connected and neither one can be understood without the other.

tion, which is an exact reproduction of it, says even more strongly: "Do not lead us into temptation."

Certainly, as St. James tells us, it is not God Who tempts, in the sense that He is not the author of the seduction worked by sin, of sin already begun. But the Biblical meaning of the word temptation is much broader; it means trial. [3]

"Trial" is ambiguous; it can turn out for the good as well as the evil of the one tempted. We ask God not to expose us to temptation, *but* if He judges it good to submit us to it, then "to deliver us from evil." "Blessed is the man who endures temptation," says St. James (1, 12), "for when he has been tried, he will receive the crown of life which God has promised to those who love him."

Ancient Doxological Conclusion

After the evocation of evil or the Evil One, it is impossible to exclaim Amen, which expresses enthusiasm and adherence. Two solutions have been found to overcome this difficulty. The Latin Church, in her Liturgy, has long made use of a development of the last petition of the Our Father: "Deliver us, Lord, from every evil." Then this petition, through the intercession of the Virgin Mary, Sts. Peter, Paul, and Andrew, and all the Saints, begged for peace, and it ended with the customary conclusion of the Orations, which calls for the Amen.

There exists a still more venerable and more universal way of leading to the Amen at the end of the Our Father. This consists in pronouncing, at the end of the Lord's Prayer, the doxology: "For the kingdom, the power, and the glory are Yours, now and for ever." This doxology is already found, at the end of the Our Father in the *Didache (Doctrine*

---

[3] It is thus that "Jesus was led into the desert by the Spirit to be tempted [put to the test] by the devil" (Mt 4, 1). The literal translation is: "to be tempted by the devil." It is the devil who tempts, but it is truly the Spirit Who submits Jesus, Who exposes Jesus, to the temptation!

of the Twelve Apostles), a Christian writing which may go back to the first century, hence not so far removed from the latest books of the New Testament.

This doxology was so widely diffused that in certain ancient manuscripts it was introduced into the very text of the Gospel. All the exegetes (professional interpreters of Scripture) agree that it is not of Biblical but of liturgical origin. It is constantly used by Eastern Christians and by Protestants.

The "Deliver us, Lord, from every evil" of our Liturgy has been simplified. There is no longer any intercession of the Saints. [4] The priest concludes the "Deliver us, Lord, from every evil" by saying that we "wait in joyful hope for the coming of our Savior, Jesus Christ," which is truly in line with the eschatological spirit of the Our Father. [5] Then the people answer with an acclamation which we will now have officially in common with our separated brethren: "For the kingdom, the power, and the glory, are Yours, now and forever."

40. THE SIGN OF PEACE AND THE BREAKING OF THE BREAD

The Meaning of Peace

The priest, in the conclusion of the Our Father, has asked God to grant us not only deliverance from all evils, but the good that includes all the others: peace. For this word, in Biblical and liturgical language, has a much wider meaning than it has in the current language of our time, although

---

[4] We may be permitted to regret the simplification in this respect. The mention of "the holy Apostles Peter and Paul and Andrew" had an ecumenical aspect, Peter and Paul evoking the Church of Rome and Andrew, the Church of Constantinople.

[5] Eschatological comes from *eschata* which means the last (times). Most of the petitions of the Our Father: "Thy kingdom come.... Give us ... our daily bread. ... And lead us not into temptation" evoke our Lord's Second Coming and the trials which will precede it.

peace expresses an ideal that in our own day is most ardently desired. The greeting *"Shalom,"* peace, which the Jews address to one another, signifies all possible prosperities. [6] We could just as well translate it as: happiness.

Likewise, the Messiah is the Prince of peace; He will bring a peace that will be total and definitive, the peace which is the great messianic gift. [7] Here also we must see in this word all possible fullness.

For the Christian, peace is a fruit of the Holy Spirit, hence an immediate effect or even, one might say, an essential attribute of charity. [8]

He who has charity, loves God, and this love establishes him in a peace that cannot be disturbed by anything. He who has charity is good, patient, indulgent; he loves to forgive, he forgets evil and hence he diffuses peace all around him. [9]

The Eucharist is the Sacrifice and the Sacrament of unity and peace. What Communion tries to effect in us is to stimulate the fervor of charity, to unite us profoundly, in Christ, with God and with our brethren. It is normal, therefore, that as Communion approaches the desire for peace should insistently come back.

After asking God for the gift of peace, the priest proposes it to all saying: "The peace of the Lord be with you always," to which the people respond: "And also with you."

---

[6] Dufour in his *Vocabulary of Biblical Theology*, at the word *peace*: "Biblical peace . . . means the well-being of daily existence, the state of a man who lives in harmony with nature, with himself, and with God; concretely, it is: blessing, repose, glory, riches, salvation, life."

[7] Cf., for example, Isaiah 9, 6-7; 32, 17-18; 60, 17-16; etc.

[8] Cf., for example, Galatians 5, 22: "The fruit of the Spirit is: charity, joy, peace, patience, kindness, goodness, faith, modesty, continency."

[9] Cf. Mt 5, 9; Lk 6, 27-36; Jn 15, 12-17; 1 Cor 13, 4-7; etc.)

Then the deacon, or the priest, if he judges it opportune, adds: "Let us offer each other the sign of peace," and the faithful manifest the fraternal charity that should reign among them by a gesture. The most common gesture is the kiss, but this varies according to times and places; sometimes it is an embrace, an accolade, a handshake, etc.

Formerly, the kiss of peace did not leave the cloister of the sanctuary. Of course, this did not mean that charity was a privilege of the clergy! But the kiss of peace came from Christ, and followed a descending order which was rather rigorously hierarchical. The priest, after kissing the altar (that is, Christ), gave the kiss of peace to the deacon, who transmitted it to the subdeacon, and so on, all along the line of ministers and servers.

Today the faithful are invited to manifest their union in charity and this shows a different view of things. Charity remains supernatural, and even sacramental. It always comes from God, Who is Love. But it does not have to follow rigorously a descending line. It springs, as it were spontaneously, from the members of the Christian community among themselves.

Breaking of the Bread

Another gesture will make this unity in charity more explicit and concrete. This is the Breaking of the Bread. In olden times it had its practical usefulness, since the faithful brought regular loaves, which had to be broken up so that everyone at Communion time would receive a mouthful. This utility has disappeared as a result of the use of "small Hosts" cut up beforehand. But the gesture of the breaking remains and it retains a twofold value.

First of all, it links us with Jesus Christ. At the Last supper, Jesus broke the bread, as He had done at the time of the multiplication of the loaves. [10] At Emmaus, the two disciples, who had remained spiritually blind so long, "recognized [Jesus] in the breaking of the bread" (Lk 24, 35). In the first Christian community, it seems certain that the "breaking of the bread" meant the Eucharistic Banquet. [11]

But this is more than just an historical souvenir no matter how touching. The Breaking of the Bread has a deep meaning of unity. No one has expressed this better than St. Paul: "The Bread that we break, is it not the partaking of the Body of the Lord? Because the Bread is one, we though many, are one body, all of us who partake of the one Bread" (1 Cor 10, 16-17).

Thus, the Breaking of the Bread and the kiss (or other gesture) of peace express the same mystery of unity in Christ and in fraternal charity. Even if the "small hosts" have been separated in advance, the fact that all who have come together communicate from Hosts which have been consecrated at the same Mass once again expresses this mystery of unity.

Signification of Unity

The concrete gesture of the breaking of the Bread has been maintained for the "large Host" of the priest. He breaks it, first of all, because he cannot put the unbroken Host directly in his mouth, and also because at this moment he accomplishes another rite, whose signification, however, is not evident.

After breaking the Host, he places one small fragment in the chalice. Why? All sorts of hypotheses have been proposed in this respect. It is useless to repeat them, for none is certain and they refer to ancient customs which have long since disappeared. Yet this gesture has been preserved in all the liturgies.

---

[10] This fact is recorded in all the accounts except that of St. John.

[11] Cf. Acts 2, 42-46; 20, 7-11; 27, 35; 1 Cor 10, 16.

In our opinion, it certainly presents a signification of unity since it unites the consecrated Bread with the consecrated Wine. Is this a way of recalling that the Christ with Whom we shall be united in Communion is now the living Christ, the Risen Christ, Whose Flesh and Blood are reunited? We have already said that the separation of the Body and the Blood of Christ on the Cross does not appear to explain validly the sacrificial character of the Eucharistic Consecration which is performed with bread and wine that are normally separated. We therefore incline to the view that this reunion of the two Eucharistic elements teaches us rather that, in reality, if we receive in Communion *either* the consecrated Bread alone, *or* the Bread *and* the Chalice, we receive in either case the whole Christ, Who is living and glorious.

This explanation does not pretend to explain the origin of the rite in question. But the origin of a rite and its historical and material cause, which might escape us, is one thing. Quite another is the signification it can have for us today in harmony with the existing liturgical context.

"The Lamb of God"

During the Breaking of the Bread the faithful chant the invocation: "Lamb of God, You take away the sin of the world: have mercy on us." They repeat this twice and the third time change the petition to: "Grant us peace." Actually, this chant was introduced into the Mass to accompany the rite of the Breaking of the Bread, which used to take much too long. Hence, it was repeated as long as necessary, and this too can be done today, notably in concelebrations comprising a large number of priests, which makes it necessary to break several large Hosts.

When the Breaking of the Bread is over, the priest, or the principal concelebrant, says in a low voice a private prayer of preparation for Communion. He is permitted to choose between two formulas, both of which express humility and confidence.

Formerly, the priest finished his preparation and then received Communion. After that ("If there are faithful who are going to Communion," said the Missal, as if such an eventuality were doubtful and of slight importance), he showed them the Body of Christ. Our new rite is much more beautiful. The last prayers of preparation are common to the priest (or the concelebrants) *and* the faithful. Are not all of them going to participate in the same Sacrifice they have offered together and receive the same Food, the One Bread, since, as St. Paul expressed it, "we, though many, are one Body," we all belong to one and the same People of God.

41. THE INVITATION TO COMMUNION

People Gradually Lost Habit of Communion

In order to give a proper explanation of the present rites of Communion we have to recall the past. After the primitive period during which most of the faithful, with the exception of penitents, received Communion every time they participated in the Mass—though at that time the Celebration took place less frequently than nowadays—the faithful gradually lost the habit of receiving Communion. Things became so bad that it was necessary for the Fourth Lateran Council, in 1215, to promulgate the precept making it obligatory for "all the faithful of both sexes who had reached the age of discretion" to receive Communion once a year.

It was not, as is frequently alleged, Jansenism that drove the faithful away from Communion. The 17th century practiced frequent Communion. If Jansenism had influence on the general practice, it ocurred as some kind of distinct after-effects only during the 19th century. But the Middle Ages had been a time during which the faithful received very infrequently. Saint Louis, who assisted at two Masses every day and at night went to assist at Matins with the Brothers Minor or Preachers, received Communion only three times a year.

But the Christian people had a veritable hunger for the Eucharist, and to satisfy this craving a poor substitute was granted them. In the year 1200 the Elevation of the Host after the Consecration was introduced in Notre Dame of Paris. To put it more exactly, in order to avoid abuses which sprang up to satisfy the disorderly desire to see the Host, the Elevation of the Host was made lawful.

The rite of the Elevation of the Chalice was begun only in the 14th century, for the sake of symmetry. Moreover, this did not elicit the same interest, since the chalice does not enable the people to see the consecrated Wine.

If, when speaking of the Consecration above, we neglected to speak about this rite of the Elevation, this was done on purpose. For this rite which the East has always ignored at this particular time of the Mass-Liturgy, is very secondary. It adds nothing to the Sacrifice. Its object is only to show the people the Bread and the Chalice after their Consecration.

Moreover, this has lost much of its interest. The practice of celebrating the Mass facing the people has brought with it a much more discreet showing of Host and Chalice. The somewhat romanticized vehemence of this showing was popularized by numerous pious pictures, stemming from the fact that the priest, who had his back turned to the people, had to raise the Host and the Chalice high above his head so that people might see them! Besides, the liturgical renewal has given back its importance, which is a primary one, to what was formerly called the "Minor Elevation," which forms the conclusion and the summit of the Eucharistic Prayer and calls for the solemn *Amen* of the people.

Only the Sick Communicated

Though the Communion of the people at Mass had become extremely rare, priests, fortunately, continued to bring Communion to the sick. No doubt, the bringing of the Viaticum that was done solemnly through the streets (with a canopy, lights, a bell) is at the origin of the "processions of the Blessed Sacrament." When Communion was given during Mass, this distribution was made in a very simple manner, since it had been prepared for by the Mass itself. But one could not give Communion to a sick person in his room without surrounding it with certain liturgical ceremonies: confession, profession of faith, showing of the Host.

When Communion was reintroduced into the Mass, it brought with it the whole ritual of Communion to the sick.

Older readers recall that it was the rule to recite the Confiteor before Communion given in Church, to which the priest answered with two prayers asking for the forgiveness of the recipients. Happily, this Confiteor or confession has been abolished. It was a strange practice, since people had already said the Confiteor at the beginning of Mass and especially since they had participated in the whole celebration of the Sacrifice.

One can understand that a sick person, seeing His Lord come to him in his poor home, might repeat the exclamation of the centurion of the Gospel: "Lord, I am not worthy that You should come *under my roof.* Speak but a word and my soul will be healed." This word applies less in reality to the Communion of the faithful present at Mass. But it does express well the sentiments of humility and faith which should animate us as we approach so great a Sacrament.

People Now Urged to Communicate

There is another enrichment of the Liturgy nowadays which is to be applauded: the priest is not content merely to distribute Communion when the moment for it has arrived. Taking the parts of his Host (with the other concelebrants holding their own in their hand), he raises them above the paten toward the faithful, saying: "This is the Lamb of God Who takes away the sins of the world." [12]

This expression is obviously connected with the chant which has invoked Jesus under the title of Lamb of God. But it is not yet an invitation to receive Communion. Hence, from now on the priest will add: "Happy are those who are called to His supper." This beautiful text is taken from the Book of Revelation. [13] It has evidently been chosen to be connected with what precedes through the theme of the Lamb.

The Eastern liturgies have an invitation which is at the same time a warning: "Holy things to the holy!" But our Liturgy does not forget to inspire us with the sentiments of humility and religious fear that should be ours at this moment: all say with the priest: "Lord, I am not worthy to receive You, but only say the word and I shall be healed."

Formerly, this declaration of unworthiness was repeated three times. Today, it is said only once. For here we have neither acclamation nor ardent petition which justifies repetition, but a statement, which would only be weakened if repeated.

The priest then receives Communion, consuming the Host he has in his hand and drinking the precious Blood. After this he takes the paten once more to bring Communion to the faithful.

---

[12] This was the description of Christ given by John the Baptist to his disciples (Jn 1, 29). The liturgical text has *peccata, sins,* in the plural. But the Gospel text is in the singular.

[13] 19, 9. This text says more precisely: "to the marriage supper of the Lamb."

42. THE COMMUNION OF THE FAITHFUL IN THE BODY OF CHRIST

Communion Procession with Song

It is proper for the faithful to go to Communion not only in good order but in a procession. This is important to the very meaning of their movement to the altar. It is not a question of going to Communion without paying attention to others, intent only on receiving Christ's Body in a selfish way. It is a question of showing that we are *one,* and that we are going to communicate together, uniting with the Body of Christ, so as to express and strengthen this unity founded on our Baptism, for this Sacrament has made us members of one single Body.

It is also proper that this unity be expressed in a song in which all join. Nothing is more dismal than a silent procession, for people on the move usually cause a hub-bub. The short sentence which the Missal calls the Communion is the antiphon which all repeated as a refrain of a Processional Psalm. Hence, a Communion Song, in one form or another, is highly recommended.

Those who complain that they are disturbed in their "recollection" no doubt have a wrong idea of what recollection means; it does not entail being absorbed in one's personal reflections, but gathering and directing our thoughts toward one same end and purpose. In any case, they have a faulty idea of Communion; if it is a profoundly personal action, it must at the same time be a manifestly community function.

Profession of Faith

But there is something still much more important: the rite of Communion given to each communicant. The one who distributes it shows the Host to the communicant raising and holding it stationary for a moment. At the same time he says: "The Body of Christ." The communicant responds: "Amen," and then receives his Lord.

Thus, only in the last few years have we seen the restoration of this very old custom which is rich in meaning. The faithful are not satisfied merely to receive and consume. Communion is a voluntary act and a theological act. What then is the meaning of this short dialogue? "Under these appearances," the priest tells the communicant, "there is truly the Body of Christ." Hence, the response means: "It is true. I am certain of it. I believe." The Amen is a *profession of faith*.

But there is more. For the "Body of Christ" does not only point to the physical presence of Christ's risen Body. It also signifies His "Body which is the Church" (Col 1, 24), the Body which has founded, but which is continued throughout history, the Body which we are and which we build up through charity.

This second meaning of "Body of Christ" has a corresponding new meaning of the "Amen" which responds to it: "Yes. By communicating in Christ's Body, I wish to contribute to the building up, and to the unity, of His Body which is the Church." And so this very short rite is at the same time a profession of faith and a promise of charity. [14]

Standing or Kneeling?

Two ways of giving and receiving Communion with the consecrated Bread have been the subject of heated discussions among Catholics.

There was first the question of receiving the Host while kneeling or standing. The first seemed to be the traditional way. But, in fact, it dates only from the Middle Ages, and it

---

[14] St. Augustine developed this theme over and over again with great depth. His splendid texts on this subject have been gathered together and printed by M. Huftier, *Corpus Christi. Amen,* in *La Vie Spirituelle* (October 1964), pp. 477-501.

was not even prescribed by the rubrics of the Missal. Evidently, kneeling visibly expresses adoration. This is almost the only advantage one could attribute to it.

To receive standing has in its favor that it is a very ancient custom and has a very beautiful significance: it recalls that we who are participating in Communion with Christ are men who have risen with Him. Moreover, the Council of Nicaea (325) had prohibited kneeling on Sundays because it is the Day of the Resurrection. Eastern Catholics have always received Communion standing.

On the other hand, this standing position has practical advantages (especially if the one who distributes Communion stands a step higher than the position of the communicant): it makes possible an orderly and quick procession of Communion. However, it is desirable that a recommendation of the *Instruction of the Eucharistic Mystery* of 1967 be observed. It asks for a gesture of respect before the reception of the Body of Christ, but this should be done "at the right time so that the order of people going to and from Communion may not be disrupted."

In any case, this *Instruction,* in the same article 34, specifies: "The faithful should willingly adopt the method [of receiving] indicated by their pastors, so that Communion may truly be a sign of brotherly union among all those who share in the same Table of the Lord."

In the Mouth or in the Hand?

Then there is the question, is it better to receive the Body of the Lord in the mouth or in the hand?

The first way is certainly the one that has been most common for many centuries in the East as well as in the West, but for different reasons. The West consecrates the Eucharist with unleavened breads which have become in our usage very light and small hosts. They cling readily to the

tongue but it is not easy to hold the small ones in one's
hand. This disadvantage disappears when a thicker unleavened bread is used and the hosts are made much larger and
solid.

In the East, people receive Communion under both species,
and generally the consecrated Bread is dipped in the consecrated wine of the chalice. This makes it necessary to place
the elements in the mouth of the communicant.

During the first centuries of the Church Communion was
received in the hand. The Fathers describe it even in detail:

> When you approach, do not come forward holding the
> palms of your hands extended, and your fingers sepa-
> rate. But, since your right hand will bear the King, make
> for Him a throne with your left hand, and in the hollow
> of your hand receive the Body of Christ and respond:
> Amen. [15]

This manner of proceeding, in our opinion, has three
advantages. It avoids the definite inconveniences presented
from the viewpoint of hygiene by placing the Host in the
mouth of the communicant. It calls forth on the part of the
communicant a more virile and less infantile attitude. Finally, though the faithful always *receives* Communion, he is
at the same time active: he *takes* the Body of Christ. [16]

Some of the faithful are afraid of touching the Body of
Christ with their hand, but is their tongue more sacred? [17]

---

[15] St. Cyril of Jerusalem, *Mystagogical Catechesis,* V, 21.

[16] The scriptural argument has no value in this case. The word of
Christ at the Last Supper is usually translated: "Take and eat." But
the translation "Receive and eat" can also be defended.

[17] The reason for such a fear is an unwritten but indelible law drum-
med into first communicants: the Host must not be touched with
one's teeth. And why not? The Fathers of the Church recommended
that even communicants chew; and without chewing one does not
really eat.

Another frequently heard argument is that only the priest can touch
the Body of Christ because his hands were consecrated with the holy
oils at his ordination (which has not always been required). But the
deacon is the normal minister of the Eucharist and yet his hands have
not received any special consecration.

The custom of giving Communion in the mouth (for it is only a custom, since we do not believe it is stipulated in any text [17a] has in its favor its relative antiquity and universality. But bishops could certainly allow the Body of Christ to be given in the hand of the faithful who express a desire for this.

We have all seen or heard of celebrations of "avant-garde" Masses in which the faithful took the consecrated "Breads" from a basket or a large platter. We do not consider this advisable—but not on account of doctrinal reasons. For even on such occasions one "receives" the Eucharist from the priest who has consecrated it.

First of all this way of acting is unhygienic: some communicants may have hands that are a bit uncertain or spotted or trembling and pick up one Host and then another. Most of all, however, this procedure suppresses freedom of choice. In this whole affair, we must insure that respect be given if not to the convictions of others at least to the reservations or sensitivities of each. If the priest himself offers the consecrated Bread, the communicant remains free to open his mouth or to extend his hand.

43. COMMUNION FROM THE CHALICE

In all the Eucharistic Prayers, which are now identical in this respect, we have our Lord say: "Take this, all of you, and eat it: this is My Body," and, with respect to the cup:

[17a] Since this was originally published, an official document on the subject has been issued by the Congregation on Divine Worship: "Instruction on the Manner of Administering Holy Communion" (May 29, 1969). After outlining the history of the methods in which Communion has been received over the years (much as is done in the text above), the document concludes that the method currently in use by which the minister places the Host on the tongue of the communicant is to be retained and to be considered as "prescribed by custom." However, it does leave the door open to the usage of placing the Host in the hand in those places where such a usage has already developed and where the Bishops' conferences deem it advisable to continue it, provided the permission of the Apostolic See is obtained. [Tr.]

"Take this, all of you, and drink from it." [18] In His discourse on the Bread of life, He had said: "Unless you eat the Flesh of the Son of Man, and drink His Blood, you shall not have life in you. He who eats My Flesh and drinks My Blood has life everlasting and I will raise him up on the last day. For My Flesh is food indeed, and My Blood is drink indeed. He who eats My Flesh, and drinks My Blood, abides in Me and I in him." [19] All ancient descriptions of the Liturgy show us the faithful eating the bread and drinking the cup. All the Eastern Catholics, and even the Anglicans and other Protestants, receive Communion under both species.

Why, then, for so many centuries, have Latin Catholics, with the exception of the celebrating priest, received Communion only under the species of Bread, seemingly disobeying the precept of our Lord and mutilating the Eucharist?

Reasons for Receiving only the Host

The explanation seems to belong to the purely practical order. It is possible that fear arose regarding the difficulty of handling the cup and the danger of spilling the Precious Blood when these were presented to large numbers and different types of the faithful. This fear became greater as devotion was directed more to the real Presence.

---

[18] It is only in the account of Matthew (26, 27) that we find the expression: "All of you drink of this." It is true that Mark says (14, 23): "They all drank of it." The words "all of you" in the expression "Take this, all of you, and eat it" are not found in any account of the Last Supper. But they are clearly implied by the fact that Jesus must have given a piece of bread to everyone, whereas He merely passed the cup around. "All of you" must have been added by the Roman liturgy because of the evident tendency to make the two consecrations as harmoniously parallel as possible.

[19] Jn 6, 53-56. The first part of this discourse (35-52) and its conclusion (v. 58) deals with bread and nothing else. But this does not exclude the wine; (there is no question of wine): for Jesus has just multiplied *loaves;* also, because He is making use of the theme of the manna; and finally because "to eat bread," among the Jews, signifies to make a meal, without excluding drink.

On the other hand, the doctrine gradually became prevalent that the Consecration was accomplished by the words. The primitive custom of "consecrating" large chalices containing wine destined for the faithful by pouring in them some drops taken from the chalice of the priest doubtless seemed a rather dubious procedure. But above all we believe that abandonment of Communion under both Species came from the general abandonment of Communion on the part of the people. As we saw in the previous chapter, the Communion of the sick received, on this account, a particular prominence. And bringing the Eucharist under the form of bread is much easier than bringing consecrated wine.

The Hussites, and then the other Protestants, have reproached Catholics for this incomplete practice. They reasoned on the basis of an overly literal fidelity to the words of the Gospel, just as Catholics on their part quoted texts in which there is question only of bread. This word bread, as we said before, means the whole repast, just as flesh and blood express in two correlative words the humanity of our Lord.

It is certain that, in olden times, if the faithful normally received Communion under both species, they had no objection to receiving under only one species. The faithful who kept the Eucharist in their homes, kept it only under the species of Bread. The acolytes who brought it to prisoners in linen bags suspended from their neck, evidently took only the Bread. On the other hand, little children who had just been baptized received Communion only under the species of wine.

Above all, Latin Catholics were reproached for reserving Communion from the chalice to priests, a practice which established a segregation within the universal priesthood. In reality, this privilege was based not only on practical reasons which we have explained, but also on a doctrinal reason: the priest, not because of his person or his dignity, but in virtue of his ministerial function, represents all the faithful.

This provided the justification for Masses in which the priest alone received Communion, a practice which was condemned by Luther not without reason but in too absolute a fashion. And in this way it was explained that the whole people received Communion from the chalice in the person of the priest.

Communion from Chalice Now Allowed

In any case, the words of our Lord and the early practice of receiving under both species cannot be denied. Hence, it is fortunate that the Second Vatican Council has once again authorized Communion for the faithful from the chalice. [20] Gradually, this permission has been extended to various categories of lay people. We need not enumerate them here. [21]

But the intention of the legislator is clear. Communion from the chalice is granted widely but not for everyone at any time; it is granted to those who participate more closely in diverse community celebrations, which, therefore, presupposes that these receive a certain preparation for it.

The Conciliar text makes it clear that this broadening retains the principles laid down by the Council of Trent, namely, that Communion under one species is always licit and does not constitute a real impoverishment of the Sacrament, for Christ is always received whole even under only one species. It makes no difference in what way theologians explain the fact. It is something that cannot be doubted by one who holds the Christian faith. [22]

---

[20] Article 55, in the *Constitution on the Sacred Liturgy* thus abrogated Canon 852 which said: "the Holy Eucharist shall be given only under the species of bread."

[21] *Instruction on the Eucharistic Mystery*, no. 32.

[22] In this regard, the theory of "concomitance" is often put forth: although the Sacrament designates only the Body in consecrating the Bread, and only the Blood in consecrating the wine, the fact that Christ is actually risen means that His Body is always "accompanied" (this is what the term "concomitance" signifies) by His Blood, Soul, and Divinity (and this holds reciprocally for the Blood). This explanation is plausible and commonly accepted, but it is not obligatory on the faithful.

Let us note in passing that Communion under the species of Wine alone is also authorized, for certain sick people who are unable to take any solid food. In this case, it is permissible, subject to the judgment of the local bishop, to celebrate Mass near the sick person. [23]

Symbolic Advantage

If we do not receive more when we receive the Bread *and* the Wine which have been consecrated than when we receive only one of the two, what advantage is there in receiving under both species?

Although there is no advantage from the standpoint of the reality contained in the Sacrament, the advantage is considerable from the standpoint of expression, and of sign; for the Sacraments are sacred realities, but at the same time also signs, testimonies, professions of faith.

In like manner, the Mass celebrated by one priest alone, with neither response nor participation on the part of the faithful, is truly the Sacrifice of Christ and the Church, but, as the common saying goes, "it does not look it." Since we are not pure spirits, we need signs to express and also to foster our faith. [24]

The *Instruction on the Eucharistic Mystery* gives a fine explanation of this expressive value (no. 32, *italics added):*

> Holy Communion considered, *as a sign, has a more perfect form* when it is received under both kinds. For under this form (leaving intact the principles of the Council of Trent, by which under either species there is received the true Sacrament and Christ whole and entire), *the sign of Eucharistic banquet* appears more perfectly. Moreover, it *shows more clearly* how the new and eternal Covenant is ratified in the Blood of Christ, as it also expresses the re-

---

[23] *Instruction on the Eucharistic Mystery,* no. 41.

[24] Cf. art. 59, *Constitution on the Sacred Liturgy.*

lation of the Eucharistic banquet to the eschatological banquet in the Kingdom of the Father. [25]

We must add that the cup also has its proper signification. In particular, it is the symbol of unity and intimacy, [26] even more than the bread which is shared, for all drink from the same cup. This symbol is especially telling when, at a wedding, husband and wife drink from the same cup.

Of course, one can raise the same objections from the standpoint of hygiene in this case as in the case of receiving the Host in the mouth. There is this difference however: Communion under the species of Bread is given to a much greater number. On the other hand, we can always dispense ourselves from receiving the cup, since we have received "Christ whole and entire" under the species of Bread.

Communion under the two species can have other methods of distribution. There is intinction which consists in giving to the faithful the Bread dipped in the Wine, a method used in the East. [27] But it is easier for those of the Eastern rites because they use leavened and more solid and thicker bread than we do.

It is also possible to receive Communion from the chalice by means of a straw or small pipe, or a spoon. But these are rarely used among us.

In any case, the priest or the deacon presents the Precious Blood saying: "The Blood of Christ" to which the communicant answers: "Amen."

---

[25] The "eschatological banquet," that is, "the end of times," is heaven seen under the image of the repast or supper in which we are the guests of God. The *Instruction* refers here to Mt 26, 26-29. Cf. also Is 25, 6; Mt 8, 11; Lk 14, 15; 22, 14-16; Rv 3, 20; 19, 9.

[26] Cf. 2 Kgs 12, 3; Pss. 16, 5; 23, 5.

[27] It is unpleasant to recall how some Latins in their polemics have gone so far sometimes as to call this intinction of the Eastern Christians "the Communion of Judas." Judas did receive a piece of bread that had been dipped (Jn 13, 26). But it had been dipped in the plate, not in the cup, and the general opinion is that Judas had left the Cenacle before the Institution of the Eucharist.

VII
CONCLUDING RITES

44. THE ABLUTIONS AND THE PRAYERS AFTER COMMUNION

After a meal at home we wash the dishes and glasses, fold napkins and clean up everything. This is also what naturally takes place after Mass, when Communion, that is, the sacred meal, is over. These utilitarian actions should be performed as discreetly as possible. Hence, it is proper to go to the credence table or to the sacristy to do these things. It is also permissible to wait until the faithful have left.

Formerly, the priest washed not only the chalice but also —on two separate occasions—his fingers which had touched the Host. This rite now is practically optional. This is logical, for the rule obliging the priest to keep his thumb and index finger joined from the Consecration until the end of the ablutions has been abolished.

This is an application of a very clear principle of Sacramental doctrine: no doubt, every time one breaks the Host, Christ is present wholly in each fragment. [1] But this does

---

[1] This is explained by the doctrine of transubstantiation. The substance (the total and fundamental being) of the Body of Christ replaces the substance of bread, without a change in the appearances. The quantitative variations of the bread do not affect, therefore, the substance of the Body of Christ. When the Host is divided, the Body of Christ is not broken or divided. As long as there is *bread*, in any quantity, there is the presence of Christ's Body.

not mean that the Host is indefinitely divisible. When the
particles are so small that they cease to appear like bread,
Christ, whose Sacramental presence is bound to the appearance of bread, disappears.

Hence, either what adheres to the fingers of the priest is
a fragment that can be recognized as bread, and he must
immediately put it on the paten; or the particles are infini-
tesimal, invisible or at least unidentifiable; in this case there
is no longer a real Presence. The washing of the hands of
the priest can have a value of respect and mark the conclusion of the sacred rite; but faith in the real Presence does
not require such an ablution.

Silent and Communal Prayer after Communion

What is much more important than these material actions
is prayer after Communion. We purposely abstain from using
the current expression of thanksgiving after Communion. [2]

This expression in fact has two drawbacks. The whole
Mass is a thanksgiving, a 'eucharist'; and Communion cannot be isolated from the Mass. This then would mean that
we give thanks for giving thanks. Besides, thanksgiving
concerns gifts already received; this certainly applies to the
incomparable Gift which is the participation in the Supper
of the Lord. But the prayer after Communion must look
rather to the future: how will my life be more Christian after this Communion? [3]

---

[2] This is in line with the *Second Instruction on the Liturgical Renewal* and the *Instruction on the Eucharistic Mystery*, respectively of
May 4 and 25, 1967. These speak only of "private prayer" or "prayer."

[3] In line with this a director of a seminary published a booklet called
Thanksgiving, in which he suggested as one of the best thanksgivings
after Communion to make or renew a spiritual resolution "just for today." [Tr.]

When the Communion is over, one can sing a hymn of thanksgiving, on condition, however, that it does not repeat the hymn in which it is desirable that all should have joined during Communion. But above all this chant should not prevent the silent prayer which the *Second Instruction on Liturgical Reform* (no. 15) has recommended.

We are still at Mass, we are still in the assembly. Hence, it is not a question so much of a private prayer, which is highly recommended, and which will take place, if possible, after the Mass. [4] The prayer we here speak of is *a silent prayer but in community.*

Too often, we have identified vocal prayer with liturgical and community prayer, and silent prayer with free and private prayer. The new rite of the Mass calls for several periods of *liturgical silence,* namely, for the Penitential Rite, after the "Let us pray" of the first Oration, and now after Communion. The faithful can then draw inspiration from the words of the Communion Song, and in particular from its antiphon, which has been proposed to all. [5]

This silent prayer after Communion ends with a community prayer expressed by the priest in the Prayer after Communion (or Postcommunion). Like the Prayer over the Gifts it is connected more with the Eucharist than with the feast of the day. It has, usually two parts: we recall the Gift we have just received, then ask that this Gift may produce its fruits in us. And here we think first about the daily life and occupations we shall once more engage in.

---

[4] *Instruction on the Eucharistic Mystery,* no. 38 .

[5] Someone might remark that a "community" silent prayer during Mass is as strange as "community meditation"; and is it necessary to entertain community thoughts even in our private prayer addressed to Christ Whom we have just received? Is not this artificially forcing ourselves to be "liturgical," social-minded, at every moment of the Mass? [Tr.]

The *Instruction on the Eucharistic Mystery* stated this very well in recommending private prayer after Communion:

> Union with Christ, to which the Sacrament itself is directed, is not to be limited to the duration of the celebration of the Eucharist; *it is to be prolonged into the entire Christian life,* in such a way that the Christian faithful, contemplating unceasingly the gift they have received, *may make their life a continual thanksgiving* under the guidance of the Holy Spirit and may produce fruits of greater charity. [6]

But the liturgical prayer after Communion looks even farther along the same line. Every Communion, and not only our last one which is a "viaticum," that is, "provision for our journey," for the last voyage, engages us, commits us on the way to eternal life.

Every Communion makes us participate in the life of God. But we shall live this life fully and openly when we

---

[6] *Instruction on the Eucharistic Mystery,* no. 38, *italics added.* We might add here the words of Pope Pius XII in his famous *Encyclical on the Sacred Liturgy (Mediator Dei)* with respect to thanksgiving *after Mass:* "When the Mass . . . is over, the person who has received Holy Communion is not thereby free from the duty of thanksgiving; rather, it is most becoming that [when this is possible, of course] [he] . . . should recollect himself and in intimate union with the Divine Master hold loving and fruitful converse with Him. Hence they have departed from the straight way of truth, who . . . assert and teach that when Mass has ended, no such thanksgiving should be added, not only because the Mass is itelf a thanksgiving but also because this pertains to a private and personal áct of piety and not to the good of the community.

"But, on the contrary, the very nature of the Sacrament demands that the reception should produce rich fruits of Christian sanctity. . . . The Sacred Liturgy of the Mass also exhorts us to do this when it bids us pray in these words: 'Grant, we beseech You, that we may always continue to offer thanks . . . and may never cease from praising You.' Wherefore . . . who would dare to reprehend or find fault with the Church, because she advises her priests and faithful to converse with the Divine Redeemer for at least a short while after Holy Communion, and inserts in her liturgical books, fitting prayers . . . by which the sacred ministers may make suitable . . . [thanksgiving] after [Mass]. . . . It is the good pleasure of the Divine Redeemer to hearken to us when we pray, to converse with us intimately and to offer us a refuge in His loving Heart" (no. 123). [Tr.]

shall have reached the end of our earthly life, each one of our many Communions marking, as it were, so many stages.

45. THE DISMISSAL (Three Forms)

Now that the liturgical service is over, the president has the function of dismissing the assembly. At the beginning of the Mass he had greeted the gathering by the invocation of the Three Divine Persons. Now he blesses it in their Name. Then he declares that the assembly is dismissed. This is all that the words, *Ite, missa est"* mean: "Go, this is the dismissal." This formula, borrowed from secular Roman customs, is somewhat dry. The liturgies of the East use: "Go in the peace of Christ."

Henceforth, we can use this expression, or "The Mass is ended, go in peace," or "Go in peace to love and serve the Lord." All respond: "Thanks be to God."

Some would have liked to have here the words: "Go on the Mission" which is not really a translation but is a good suggestion as far as its content is concerned. For the Christian who has participated in the Sacrifice of his Lord, which was offered for the salvation of men, and offered with the Church which is the Sacrament of salvation for the world, cannot be content with just going back home, satisfied for having accomplished his duty and obeyed the law. Without transforming himself into a missionary or a preacher, he must try to radiate justice and charity around him. [7]

The dismissal, as presently given, has no variants. If the Mass is followed by another liturgical function, then, of course, the faithful are not dismissed. On such occasions one says simply: "Let us bless the Lord," and all answer: "Thanks be to God."

---

[7] The last English option ("Go in peace to love and serve the Lord") is the equivalent of this suggestion. [Tr.]

Finally, these conclusions are omitted if the Mass is celebrated for a funeral, and followed by the "commendation and final farewell," for the latter is a blessing destined for the body of the deceased.

We hope the reader will excuse us for ending our explanation with such minutiae. They express the will of the Council, and have a place in that whole reform: to make easier the participation of the faithful in the Mass by a simplification of the rites, rendering clear each one in itself and in its connection with the ensemble.

CONCLUSION

46. WILL THERE BE MORE CHANGES IN THE MASS?

We have finished the task we had undertaken: to explain the Mass as it will appear today. People who always want completeness will have remarked that certain things were missing in our present work. We have spoken only of the most important gestures of the priest. Others have no particular meaning; they belong to the style of the Celebration.

We have also left aside some secondary prayers of the priest. Some formerly found in the Missal have disappeared. Others still remain and are said in a low voice, as before. But now that important parts such as the Prayer over the Gifts and the Eucharistic Prayer are no longer said in a low voice, the somewhat paraliturgical character of these prayers of devotion has become evident.

Liturgy No Longer Frozen

Soon after the end of the Council, the Mass began to undergo diverse changes, but these were partial and successive. Some must have given the impression of being abrupt, harsh and disorderly. In reality, it was a question of a general revision of the Liturgy that would follow a general plan.

However, some changes have taken place more quickly than had been expected. One or other reform which was judged very mild called forth other unexpected and urgent ones. Some improvements which seemed to offer no difficulty were delayed because they required indispensable technical adjustments. Finally, translations and publications require time.

While one parish adopted the new rites or ways as soon as they appeared (not to speak of parishes in which such things were done in advance), the neighboring parish did not seem to be aware of the existence of new rules and rites. In one parish, the suppressions, the additions, and adaptations were prepared for, announced, and explained. In another, they were put into practice without any explanation, and when people challenged the priest, he might answer: "That's the way it is now!" and/or "We obey the Pope."

It is understandable that some of the faithful even with the best intentions in the world, found the going of "Peter's bark" jerky, uncertain, and even somewhat anarchical. Can we now tell them that all the trouble is over, everything is regulated, and the Liturgy will not be changed for some four hundred years? (This is the length of time which separates the present cataclysm from the founding of the Congregation of Rites, which contributed so well to the freezing and solidifying of the Liturgy.)

We must be cruel and answer that the Liturgy will have more changes, that in fact it will continue to change! Certainly, the general revision demanded by the Council is almost finished with respect to the Ordinary of the Mass. But if, after emerging from one frozen immobility we made sure to get into another, the renewal of the Liturgy would be a failure. In a short time—and things are moving fast nowadays—it would again become out-dated and the participation of the faithful would once again be paralyzed.

In addition we must say that from today on, the Liturgy is changing, in other words, it is mobile. Formerly, in the Latin Church, everyone, in all circumstances, had to observe exactly the same rules. An Abbey Church or a Cathedral, a parish in the suburbs or a village, a chapel of a Sisters' convent, a mission station—all had to follow the same ceremonial in principle. The "sung Mass" formed one unit, the "low Mass" another.

Living Liturgy Sought

This is no longer true today. In obedience to the new rules, we are allowed to sing according to our wishes this or that part of the Mass. If we do not sing, such a processional chant will be omitted except for the antiphon. The priest remains free to choose from among the four Eucharistic

Prayers; he can choose in the Lectionary any Reading which seems important and which had been omitted because of the occurrence of some feast; he is permitted to say another Collect than the Collect of the day; if he celebrates with a small group, he can simplify certain things somewhat.

If the Ordinary of the Mass remains a rather stable framework, this is not to say that, at least in some countries, no new Eucharistic Prayers will be created.

The liturgical texts we now have, especially the Prefaces and the Prayers, are too strictly and narrowly inspired by Latin models passed on to us from ancient times. After being satisfied for a while with simple translations sometimes slightly adapted, why will there not come a time when new Prefaces will be created, new Prayers, new Hymns that are more original, and more in harmony with the concerns and the sensibility of our time?

This is not an announcement of perpetual hurricanes and anarchical "confrontations." This evolution of forms must be done in continuity with the ancient forms and under the control of the authority responsible for unity. This is true tradition, which does not consist in blindly preserving things, but in evolving in an organic way.

If our Liturgy were afflicted with a new sclerosis, if it refused to adapt itself to the needs of men, if it were looked upon as having fallen from heaven, it would then no longer express the life of the Church. For it would no longer be docile to the inspirations of the Spirit, about Whom it is said "no one knows where He comes from nor where He is going." But He knows it well, and we must put our confidence in Him, in a spirit of unwavering docility to the Church.

Our new Eucharistic Prayers call the Mass a "living Sacrifice" or offering. May they remain alive, living, not in virtue of the caprice of men or a mania for change, but in virtue of a true faithfulness to the calls of our time as well as to the Law of the Gospel.

INDEX

(The numbers refer to the pages on which texts or words are found)

188

History (Economy) of salvation,
69, 90, 121, 122, 134, 149
Holy Spirit, 35, 136, 140
Homily, 83
Hour of Jesus, 127

Imposition of hands, 141
Incensing, 34, 106
Intercession of Saints, 110, 146
Intinction, 178

Labor, 102
Lamb of God, 164, 168
Language of Bible, 84
Last Supper, 54, 101, 123, 126,
162
Lectionary, 65, 76, 79, 80, 81, 84,
115
Lectors, 28
Liturgy (ends of), 19
Liturgy, restoration and renew-
al, 5, 186

Maledictions (Imprecations), 72
Manna, 61
Mass, 53
Mediation of Christ, 47, 121, 153
Mementos, 91
Missal, 14, 15
Monitions, 28, 85-86
Multiplication of loaves, 54, 60,
102, 163
Mystery of Faith, 57, 90, 132
Mystery, Paschal, 11, 128, 129

Offering, sacrificial, 135
"Offerre," 98
Offertory, 99
Old Testament, 66-71
Orations, 45

Participation, active, 24, 46
Passion, 126
Paten, 100
Peace, sign of, 158, 160

People of God, 9, 16, 23
(See Assembly, Church)
Pericope, 82
40, 91
Prayer, Universal (cf Faithful),
Pray, Let us, 44-45
Preface, 118, 133, 153
Presences of Christ, 19, 70
Presence, Real, 21, 180
Presence, total, of Christ under
each species, 177
Presidency, 18
President of the liturgical as-
sembly, 22
Priest, 18, 20, 22, 30, 125, 127
Priesthood of the Baptized, 22,
44, 92, 132
Psalms, 20, 71

Recapitulation, 151

Sacrifice, 21, 34, 125-130, 135
Sacrifice, heavenly, 121
Saints, intercession, 110, 146
Sanctuary, 16-17
Saturday evening (for Mass), 12
Sign, sacramental, 8, 177
Silence, 38, 39, 46, 180
Sin, 38-40
Symbol of Faith, 2, 89
Synoptics, 80

Tables (the two), 58
Thanksgiving (eucharist), 118-
122, 147, 180
Transubstantiation, 179
Trinity, 34-35

Unity, 30, 161, 162, 169, 171, 177

Washing of hands, 107
Word of God, 20, 53-83
Work and Daily life, 21, 47, 86-
87, 94 102-103, 182-183

Missals for the People ...

Countless numbers of Catholics have
found their own Missal to be ...

easier to use

far more legible

and more dignified

than leaflets or sheets distributed to the congregation.

Your own Missal will give you a better understanding of the whole mystery of salvation and
enable you to participate fully at every Mass.

The New St. Joseph SUNDAY MISSAL and Hymnal

New revised edition with ALL Official Mass texts for Sundays and Holydays. Includes the New American Version of
the Epistles and Gospels with short helpful explanations.
People's responses clearly indicated with heavy print.
Large selection of popular hymns ideal for congregational
singing.

No. 826/04—Durable paper cover .... $ .95

No. 826/67-B—Black leatherette, hard cover 1.50

No. 826/67-W—White leatherette, hard cover 1.50

THE NEW ORDER OF MASS

Handy booklet in pocket or purse-size with the official
text of the New Order of Mass with all people's responses
in heavy print. Easy-to-use at every Mass. 48 pages.

No. 47 .... **$.20**